MAD ABOUT MOVIES #8; Editors—Gary J. Svehla and Susan Svehla; Graphic Design Interior—Gary J. Svehla; Cover Design—Susan Svehla; Copy Editor—Susan Svehla; Contributing Writers—Nick Anez and Gary J. Svehla; Acknowledgments—Warner Home Video; Fox Home Video; Universal Home Video; Bender Helper Publicity; Scott Essman; Publisher—Midnight Marquee Press, Inc.

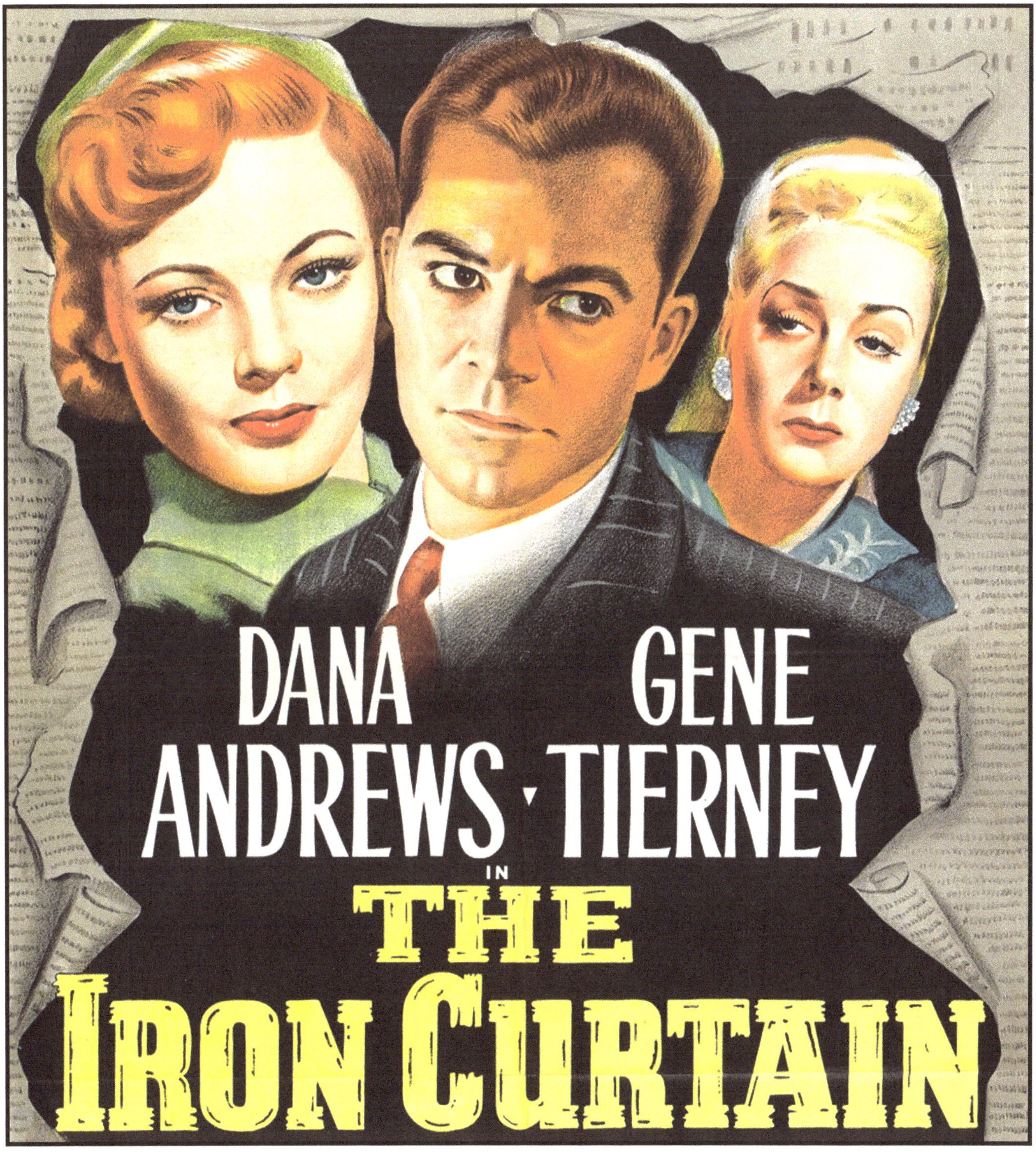

Mad About Movies Number 8
March 2011
Copyright © 2011 by Gary J. Svehla

Published irregularly for $10 per issue by Midnight Marquee Press, Inc.

Articles and art should be transmitted electronically and will remain the property of the writer/artist and copyright holder, who will retain the rights. If material intended for publication is sent to us via regular mail, it is the sender's responsibility to include return postage. No responsibility is taken for unsolicited material.

Editorial views expressed by writers are not necessarily those of the publisher, Midnight Marquee Press. Nothing from the magazine may be reproduced or shared in any media without the expressed written permission of the publisher. The Midnight Marquee Press offices are located at: 9721 Britinay Lane, Parkville, MD 21234; website: http://www.midmar.com; e-mail: midmargary@aol.com

Letters of comment addressed to Midnight Marquee or Susan and Gary Svehla will be considered for publication, unless the writer requests otherwise.

Letters of comment are encouraged; please send all comments to midmargary@aol.com and label your comments "Comments for Mad About Movies #8." Or you may send a letter to our editorial address.

We are always looking for new writers to submit articles. Please discuss any article suggestions first with Gary J. Svehla at midmargary@aol.com and check the Style Sheet link on our website to get ideas of style and formatting. Length of articles may vary. We take them long and short. Remember, our emphasis is mainly on the classics of the Golden Age, but our definition of classic and Golden Age is not based upon specific decades or year of production necessarily. Instead it's the artistic content that reflects the heart and style of classic cinema.

Copies are mailed, within the USA, for the cost of the issue plus $1 for Media Mail; $6 for Priority Mail. Issues are sent in sturdy envelopes so they should arrive at your home in near mint condition. Foreign orders are welcome, but shipping costs vary. Check with us for pricing. We accept all credit cards, PayPal, checks and money orders.

Table of Contents

2   *Mad About Movies* Editorial
     by Gary J. Svehla

3   Gordon Scott and Tarzan's Greatest Adventures
     by Gary J. Svehla

12   Dana Andrews: The Consummate Professional
     by Nick Anez

25   *Mad About Movies* Book Reviews
     by Gary J. Svehla

27   *Mad About Movies* DVD Reviews
     by Gary J. Svehla

MAD ABOUT MOVIES EDITORIAL

Welcome to issue #8 of *Mad About Movies*, our second all-color issue presented in our new format. Letters and emails have been slow trickling in, so hopefully our new look is to the liking of our readership. We do want to hear from you!

One of the most radical changes to affect home video has been the introduction of the so-called MOD or made-on-demand DVDs, glorified DVD-Rs, where major studios open up their vaults to release less-than-classic titles that otherwise might never see the light of day. Most of these titles are sold for $20 plus shipping, but Warner Bros. has caused a controversy by introducing what they label "re-mastered" titles, selling for $25. Strange that most of these titles were never released before the re-mastered version appeared. The fear is that Warner Bros. is testing the waters to raise all their MOD titles to the "re-mastered" pricing. Remember, in the past Warner Bros. released classic movie box sets where the cost of individual films was about $7 a pop. Now classic movies cost $20, and the threat of paying another five dollars is very off-putting. MOD is a new concept, a new way of marketing DVD titles, and the companies need to nurture customer support, not alienate it after only one year of operation.

Being a POD (print-on-demand) small press publisher, I more than understand the economics of having to charge a higher price for less mainstream product. Let's face it, Warner Bros. can release *The Maltese Falcon* and be guaranteed of selling thousands of copies, so they can afford to sell such titles for well below $20. When it comes to less desirable Westerns, mysteries, melodramas or film noir titles, movies that might sell 500 units total, the manufacturing cost per title is bound to be higher, so the list price must be higher. For example, a softcover book published by Midnight Marquee or McFarland, earmarked for a limited market, will list price for more than a mass market softcover book published by mainstream St. Martins. Manufacturing for a niche market necessarily means a higher per unit cost. A jump from $7 to $20 a movie is tough but digestible, but not so an increase to $25. The old adage "what the market will bear" is quite applicable here. Fans, during the first year of operation, have supported the MOD DVD market, although with more than a little grousing. However, a move to increase pricing by an additional $5 might be the straw that breaks the camel's back. The niche market consumer has embraced MOD DVDs, making them both profitable and the big buzz of the hobby for the past 12 months. But upping the price by five dollars is not the type of thank you the fan deserves. People have more than met the MOD manufacturers half way. Now it is time for the DVD companies to show their appreciation by continuing to expand availability of titles and by keeping the pricing fair. In such a situation, it's a win-win for everyone.

This issue we again feature prolific Nick Anez who does a smash up job of profiling the career of under-appreciated Dana Andrews. Anez reminds the reader that Andrews was never nominated for an Academy Award. And the actor's range—from Westerns, to film noir, from horror/suspense to melodrama—made him worthy of award consideration. From *Laura* to *Curse of the Demon* to *The Ox-Bow Incident* to *The Best Years of Our Lives*, Dana Andrews was the consummate professional.

Also, now that Warner Archive Collection has released all the Gordon Scott Tarzan movies as MOD titles, I thought it was about time for a full series analysis of the six Tarzan movies that Gordon Scott made between 1955 to 1960. From the low-budget black-and-white *Tarzan's Hidden Jungle,* to the colorful, on-location and lush *Tarzan the Magnificent,* I try to make the case that Gordon Scott is the definitive movie Tarzan.

Once again, I thank our readers for their support and we hope to continue publishing a hard copy magazine for as long as economics allow. But your continued support is essential to meet that goal!

Gary Svehla

GORDON SCOTT AND TARZAN'S GREATEST ADVENTURES

by Gary J. Svehla

Johnny Weissmuller might be the definitive Tarzan of the movies, but for baby boomers, Gordon Scott is our generation's Tarzan and the jungle hero that fueled our childhood thirst for action cinema between 1955 and 1960, when Scott starred in six Tarzan feature films (actually five, but we will discuss that one anomaly later). Discovered by Tarzan franchise producer Sol Lesser while serving as a pool lifeguard, Gordon Scott succeeded Lex Barker as the franchise Tarzan, the man who succeeded Johnny Weissmuller, the most renowned king of the jungle. While Weissmuller and Barker were naturally handsome in their under-dressed costuming, Gordon Scott became the first beefcake Tarzan, his buff and pumped-up body seeming more appropriate for playing Hercules or Goliath (indeed after his run as Tarzan, Scott traveled to Europe to appear in a string of sword-and-scandal epics). Scott transformed Tarzan into a muscle building iconic jungle hero.

I truly believe that Scott's final two runs as Tarzan—*Tarzan's Greatest Adventure* and *Tarzan the Magnificent*—are not only Scott's best Tarzan pictures but also the two greatest Tarzan movies ever produced. And when Scott, at the height of his physical prowess, was replaced by the scrawny Jock Mahoney (he played a villain in Scott's final Tarzan movie), the series never fully recovered, even though a long line of actors donned the loincloth and attempted to add vitality to the now anemic series.

Gordon Scott's Tarzan journey began with a lackluster entry that was juvenile fun yet mediocre in just about every aspect. In 1955 Scott debuted with *Tarzan's Hidden Jungle*, a B black-and-white production released by RKO. Made on a modest budget with lots of location jungle footage added to the set-bound production, Gordon Scott impresses not just with his well-manicured body and youthful appearance, but also with his overall likeability and innocence. In *Tarzan's Hidden Jungle* Zippy the chimp plays Cheta, the only family Tarzan appears to have. What boosters this movie is its excellent supporting cast. Peter van Eyck plays the self-sacrificing jungle doctor Celliers, with lovely (and soon to be Mrs. Gordon Scott, although only briefly) Vera Miles supporting van Eyck as the doctor's nurse Jill. Charles Fredericks is villain De Groot, while familiar Western character actor Jack Elam plays equally slimy bad guy Burger.

Tarzan's Hidden Jungle could have been endorsed by PETA—Gordon Scott's Tarzan lives to protect the jungle wildlife, bemoaning the fact that man is the only animal who lives to kill. Hired hunters De Groot and Burger are unable to supply the animal carcasses required by their boss, because the animals have migrated to the other side of the river, which is Sukulu country, considered taboo. Anyone who harms even a single animal is killed by the animal-protecting tribe. Of course Tarzan and Dr. Celliers are welcomed by the chief and his people. Nasties De Groot and Burger pretend to be wildlife photographers and ask the good doctor if they can accompany him to visit Sukulu country and film the self-sacrificing work he performs for both the natives and animals. The doctor refuses, but nurse Jill persuades him. Of course the villains are planning to herd the animals to the other side of the river, where hunting is allowed. When this treachery is discovered, the doctor and Jill are sentenced to death by jungle law (the tribe assumes their complicity in working with the white hunters), and are thrown into the lion's den, and not even Tarzan can save them. At least not immediately. The charging

out-of-control animals are in the process of crossing the river, when Tarzan, swinging his way to the Sukulu border, gives his dramatic jungle yell and turns them about, forcing them to return to safety. In a rather violent sequence for juvenile cinema, our two villains are crushed under the stampeding hooves of angry elephants. Tarzan returns to the tribe, jumps down into the lion's den, yells the jungle lingo that all Tarzan fans are familiar with and saves his friends and the day.

Tarzan's Hidden Jungle is never truly original and the patched together clumsy editing of location photography and studio-bound jungle sets grates. But the sympathetic portrayal of Tarzan by Scott makes the movie watchable. Let's just say that *Tarzan's Hidden Jungle* suggests better movies to come.

Next up we have the so-called anomaly feature, *Tarzan and the Trappers*, not actually a theatrical release but an aborted television series. After *Tarzan's Hidden Jungle*, producer Sol Lesser came up with the idea of a TV series, and a few episodes were filmed but never sold. So by 1958 those three aborted TV episodes were re-edited into a 70-minute feature, resembling *Tarzan's Hidden Jungle* but without the star talent. This has to be Gordon Scott's Tarzan nadir, but the truth can now be told... the patched together feature is just as entertaining (and flawed) as Scott's debut as the jungle ape man.

What we have is actually three story threads combined into one. The first and shortest component is Tarzan's family life in the jungle, where he cohabitates with jungle mate Jane (Eve Brent) and son Tartu (Rickie Sorensen). In these framing stories, Jane teaches Boy to read *Treasure Island*, and Tarzan of course chimes in that "doing" is more important than "reading." Of course Jane gets herself into all sorts of jams with poisonous snakes that curl over her lovely exposed legs, with Cheta saving her in the nick of time. Such domestic sequences seem to ground Gordon Scott's Tarzan as a protective family man, who is more domestic than he appeared to be in *Tarzan's Hidden Jungle*. While this jungle family would vanish in the next Gordon Scott entry, it would return intact in the following feature.

The second story seems a rebooting of the debuting Gordon Scott Tarzan movie, with animal trappers moving into the jungle and shooting and capturing defenseless animals. We have Lesley Bradley and Maurice Marsac as the hunters, who quickly amass numerous crates filled with jungle beasts. When Tarzan interferes, the hunters capture and cage Tartu, demanding Tarzan allow them safe passage out of the jungle or the boy will die. Of course Tarzan, working in cahoots with Cheta, undermines the hunters' work, releasing animals from cages, and of course, freeing Tartu. Gordon Scott, always lurking overhead and smiling down knowingly, makes his task seem too obvious and easy. Perhaps in such a juvenile adventure we don't want to frighten children too much, but the movie creates very little sense of impending danger. And without featuring star talent of the Jack Elam variety, the villains seem second rate and flat.

Much better is the third story thread, a redoing of *The Most Dangerous Game*. Here two villains with radically different agendas clash. The one villain Lapin (William Keene) wants to capture Tarzan, because Tarzan knows the location of the treasure of a lost jungle city. Lapin does not know what the treasure is, but treasure is treasure and he must have it. The other villain is Sikes (Saul Gorse), a long and lanky jungle hunter whose brother, admittedly a stupid brother, was sent up the river by Tarzan. Sikes feels he must avenge his brother by tracking down Tarzan, proving that he and not Tarzan is the king of the jungle and that he's the best hunter out of the two. Unfortunately, Gorse is a very bad actor that delivers his stark dialogue in an affected manner, rather overly melodramatic. The man lacks the acting chops to deliver his lines realistically. At this point in time John Carradine would have been the perfect actor

Vera Miles, Gordon Scott and Cheta from *Tarzan's Hidden Jungle*

Carl. The safari is not exactly the traditional safari. Instead, they are a bunch of hard-partying upper crust Brits who fly in their private airplane to attend an African wedding, but when pelicans swarm the plane's engines, the engines fail and the plane goes down. Of course Tarzan and companion Cheta are nearby to get the barely ruffled passengers out of the craft before it plummets over the side of an embankment, tumbling and smashing hundreds of feet below. Yolande Donlan does a particularly effective job of conveying the always slightly buzzed demeanor of the party, and her performance is quite effective.

The stark color photography is used to perfection with many night sequences being either inky black or framed with an eerie blue hue. When the Oparian natives appear, they are wearing purple paint on their forearms, shoulders and middle legs, making their appearance almost glow-in-the-dark creepy. Also the village sequence with its drawbridge, huts and sacrificial altar is always filmed colorfully (although here and in a few other sequences the studio-bound sets undermine the location photography of the African continent), and once the village is set ablaze, the color is that much more dazzling.

Basically, the movie's plot is simple yet quite effective. Tarzan, rescuing the five-person party, leads them out of the jungle to safety, since their airplane is damaged beyond repair. Hawkins, another jungle savior, appears to be just as friendly and jungle-savvy as Tarzan, but in truth plans to sell the party to the Oparian tribe, who want white sacrifices for their god. Since Hawkins has eyes for the beautiful and young Diana (who is experiencing marital problems with her hubby), he plans to substitute Tarzan as the fifth white sacrificial victim so he can claim Diana. Along the trek we encounter all sorts of jungle dangers including crocodiles who intrude when Diana is swimming in the river, etc. Finally, at the climax, Hawkins reveals his cards when the tribe overruns the white explorers and takes them back to their village. Tarzan, using Cheta's enhanced thinking skills, is able to set the village ablaze, rescue the party and get them across the about-to-burn drawbridge before it collapses. Hawkins, now the enemy of the tribe, dangles from the bridge as a spear from an irate native rams his back, causing the evil hunter to fall to his death. Of course all the safari members are safe and continue on their way back home once Tarzan points them in the right direction.

As directed by veteran H. Bruce Humberstone, the movie is acted and directed effectively and paced with just enough characterization

to bring this character to life. Tarzan, invited to come into their jungle camp, does so willingly, and he mangles henchmen and jungle natives alike. He even wrestles a big goon hired by Sikes and Tarzan easily snaps his neck in a rather violent sequence. Even when Tarzan is netted and chained, he slips out of the shackles, runs amok and disposes of the villains easily. If the movie had better fluency in the editing and a stronger cast of actors, it might have surpassed *Tarzan's Hidden Jungle*. But *Tarzan and the Trappers* still demonstrates Gordon Scott's remarkable physical performance as Tarzan. Yet these initial low-budget black-and-white programmers were only warming up for the better Scott Tarzan movies to come.

By 1957, the evolution of the Gordon Scott/Sol Lesser Tarzan series was underway. *Tarzan and the Lost Safari*, the very first Gordon Scott Tarzan film I saw theatrically, raised the bar for all those that followed. First, the movie was filmed (at least partially) in Africa and photographed in vibrant Eastman Color. The supporting cast was filled to the gills with a strong set of British veterans. Here the members of the lost safari include Robert Beatty as tracker/hunter Hawkins, Yolande Donlan (the talented wife of director Val Guest) as Gamage, Betta St. John as sexy Diana, Wilfrid Hyde-White as Doodles, Peter Arne as Diana's husband Dick and George Coulouris as

and drama to maintain even juvenile interest. Sometimes the actual location shots showing animals in their native habitat become excessive and slow the pacing to a crawl for a few moments, but the film's rhythm is a virtue overall.

Gordon Scott, buffed and very tan with his well-coiffured hair, speaks marginally, but even in simplistic phrases he conveys stoic wisdom. His jungle stunts of climbing, swinging and fighting are exceptional for the time, and his Tarzan commands attention. He is never afraid to swing down from vines above, diving headlong into a group of natives, knocking them all to the ground and rising up rapidly to continue the fight. The budget of *Tarzan and the Lost Safari* is heads and tails superior to all the Gordon Scott Tarzan movies that came before, and the film benefits from the African location filming, the Eastman Color photography, the expanded and visually interesting setpieces and the improved costuming.

By the time of this release, Gordon Scott was getting noticed and his Tarzan series was revitalizing the franchise for a brand new generation of youngsters and adults alike. As a child, when I swam in my three-foot deep above ground pool, I imagined I was Tarzan swimming across a river in Africa.

One year later, in 1958, producer Sol Lesser and director H. Bruce Humberstone returned with *Tarzan's Fight for Life*, a different take on the Tarzan universe, but one slightly inferior to *Tarzan and the Lost Safari* in some ways. Once again the MetroColor is intense and very gaudy, approximating the look of Technicolor on a budget, but the color photography is far less imaginative here! Gordon Scott never looked better. His barrow chest is more naturally musculatured and his physical presence has never been more dominating. In many ways Tarzan plays a slightly smaller role in this film, and the film's plot, until the action starts, is perhaps too complex for the programmer it is. We have dedicated Dr. Sturdy (Carl Benton Reid) and his equally dedicated but always frightened nurse Ann (Jill Jarmyn) running a medical clinic in the darkest part of Africa. The doctor is making headway with the primitives, but their witchdoctor Futa ((James Edwards), working in cahoots with warrior Ramo (a buffed Woody Strode), feels threatened by white man's medicine and undermines the efforts of the clinic. The child jungle chief-to-be is more willing to accept modern medicine, but he suffers from a dangerous fever that threatens to kill him. So the tribal medicine, as administrated by Futu, is pitted against the white man's medicine, as administered by Dr. Sturdy. If the tribe turns against modern medicine, Dr. Sturdy must abandon his jungle hospital, in fear of his life.

Tarzan gets involved because he supports progressive medicine, especially when his lovely mate Jane (Eve Brent) is stricken with appendicitis and needs immediate surgery. Tartu (Rickie Sorensen), Tarzan's adopted son, is also back from his role in *Tarzan and the Trappers*, and Jane's medical crisis provides plenty of drama (Tarzan has to save Jane from a lethal snake and circumvent a majestic waterfalls in a canoe en route to the hospital). Futu even places one of the native clinic workers under a trance to strangle Jane to death with a jungle medallion, but of course he fails. But the prolonged suspense generated by not knowing when the kindly assistant will strike is one of the film's greatest strengths.

The movie's climax involves Ramo's stealing the white man's medicine, in this case a vial of deadly poison. Ramo gives the vial to Futa so he can use modern medicine to augment his magic potions as witchdoctor, becoming a hero by saving the future tribal leader and also solidifying his position as chief "doctor" of the jungle, undermining all the work that Dr. Sturdy and his understudy Dr. Warwick (Harry Lauter) provide. Tarzan, under penalty of death, ventures into the jungle to save the young chief. It is only here, in the latter part of the film, that Gordon Scott assumes the over-the-top dynamics that we expect from a screen Tarzan. Unfortunately, he is overcome, captured, and has his outstretched arms tied to thick wooden poles. This image became the dominant one used on all the film's posters, and it shows both his rage and his untapped powers. Every child in the audience knows that Tarzan will break free from his bondage. Tied to a rack in the lion's den awaiting his heart being cut out as part of the tribal sacrifice, Tarzan slips out of his straps and pretends to still be securely bound. But at the right moment

he breaks loose and the lion, now free, attacks and kills Ramo, who dies a slightly less-than-dramatic death. Of course the witchdoctor does not believe that the white man's medicine is poison, so he drinks it himself, and dies a more fitting and tortured death. But receiving the proper medication, the young tribal chief recovers and proves the validity of modern Western medicine.

While *Tarzan and the Lost Safari* had a much better final setpiece and dramatic ending (the village goes up in flames while a drawbridge collapses, native spears flying all the time) than *Tarzan's Fight for Life*, both suffer from obvious use of studio sets. Both films contain actual stock African jungle photography, but both films use studio-created sets that undermined the potential of actual African jungle sets. *Tarzan's Fight for Life* contains less action but more drama, with less inspired photography and a more boilerplate jungle screenplay. But even all this could be compensated for with more dramatic Tarzan sequences, and far too much time is spent with Cheta, Jane and Tartu (even though the trek to the medical facility, filled with drama and tension, is quite worthy). While *Tarzan and the Lost Safari* was populated with excellent British performers, *Tarzan's Fight For Life* is filled with less spectacular American ones (although seeing the always delightful Harry Lauter is a treat), and this becomes another flaw. However, while a notch below its predecessor, *Tarzan's Fight for Life* remains an entertaining Gordon Scott Tarzan entry.

By 1959, five years into Gordon Scott's six-year run as Tarzan, Gordon Scott starred in one of the two greatest Tarzan movies ever made, *Tarzan's Greatest Adventure*, directed (and co-scripted) by John Guillermin (who also directed *The Blue Max*, *The Towering Inferno* and the 1976 *King Kong*), who was at the pinnacle of his creative powers. Also, Sol Lesser was out as producer and Sy Weintraub took over the series, producing the first of two classic Gordon Scott Tarzan entries and the best two Tarzan movies ever produced. Weintraub brought the franchise to Paramount from MGM and the budgets appear to have been increased. Besides Gordon Scott's intelligent and articulate buffed jungle hero, the cast

Tartu (Rickie Sorensen), Tarzan (Gordon Scott) and Jane (Eve Brent) are a family from *Tarzan's Fight for Life*.

was anchored with solid United Kingdom talent including Anthony Quayle, Niall MacGinnis (Karswell from *Curse of the Demon*) and Sean Connery. Once again, as *Tarzan and the Lost Safari* proved, when Gordon Scott works with a strong supporting cast, the tubocharged dramatics and character interaction make for a better movie.

The film's success is due to a taut script, cracking with suspense, but one driven with many facial close-ups delving into character, becoming almost a psychological drama for the troubled villains as they cruise down the river to confront the horror of their tortured souls. The story starts off with our band of cutthroats, including leader Slade (Quayle), O'Bannion (Connery) and Kruger (MacGinnis), disguised as natives, robbing an English settlement of dynamite, killing many of the innocents caught off guard (Slade even shoots one man in the back). One surviving witness hears one dying man cry "Slade" and Tarzan remembers that name from his past, With quiet determination, Tarzan pats Cheta good-bye and paddles off down the river to track down the murderers. In a more adult production, Tarzan is better off without Jane, Tartu and Cheta. With succinct dialogue, we learn that Slade sacrificed the lives of his party to hunt and kill a rogue elephant. Tarzan claims the jungle is only big enough for one of them. So right from the beginning Tarzan makes it clear his will be a life-or-death struggle to regain control of his jungle world. Of course gutsy and emancipated Angie (Sara Shane) crash-lands her plane alongside the river and Tarzan has to take her along on his journey, and the two slowly fall prey to romantic inclinations that are never fully explored. Perhaps the screenwriters were aware that franchise fans might remember Jane from the previous production. Tarzan obviously does not.

Meanwhile on the always too-cramped cabincruiser, barely staying ahead of Tarzan and Angie, the audience in short order learns what psychological baggage drives these cutthroats. Scarfaced leader Slade is a man who loves to see people suffer and die, and his goal is to find a cave of diamonds that will make him rich. Flunky O'Bannion is a hard-drinking, wisecracking accomplice who is quick to find flaws with the rest of the gang. Kruger, the tubby, unfit German member, likes to shave his face constantly and adjust his thick wire glasses, always working with a prop when he delivers his dialogue, his lines consisting of trying to convince Slade how

In Tarzan's *Fight for Life*, Tarzan sees to the medical needs of Jane.

much he needs this girly man on his mission. Kruger is the diamond expert and he knows which diamonds in the rough are the most valuable. The final members of the gang are sexy, sun-bathing Toni (Scillia Gabel), here for eye candy alone, and not-long-for-life Dino (Al Mulock), a man who dies in the jungle quicksand, his grasping arm emerging from the murk, a locket hanging from the branch just out of his reach. But Mulock will return in the next entry portraying a different character!

The movie shines in its suspenseful action sequences, succeeding because of expert direction. In the first extended sequence, Tarazan has Angie throw a rock across the embankment, drawing gunfire from the ambush-ready gang, as Tarzan retaliates using his knife but mostly a bow and arrow, climbing into the camouflaging trees above. However, Tarzan is no match for the sticks of dynamite that Kruger throws at his perch in the trees, knocking the jungle man to the ground, bloodying his ribs and side. Of course Angie is always lurking nearby to assist him and bandage his wounds. The death of O'Bannion is one of the movie's best sequences, as the energetic Sean Connery does a little jig daring Tarzan to take him out. Tarzan, propped behind a rock with his bow and arrow, first needs to divert the man's attention so he can jump into the open to get a clear shot at his rifle-wielding opponent. When Tarzan gets that extra step on O'Bannion, we first see the all-knowing fear in the victim's eyes just as Tarzan releases the arrow, piercing the man's chest and killing him instantly. Surprisingly Gordon Scott's Tarzan did not utilize the bow and arrow in earlier productions, but here he seems the master of the weapon and his use of it only adds dramatic tension to the proceedings.

Similar sequences occur in the eerie under-lit diamond cave as Kruger, a true sneak, makes his play to throw Slade down the deep, dark shaft to his death, but the wily villain is able to use his metal noose weapon, made to kill Tarzan, as a means of hanging on to the side of the rocky ledge. When Slade eventually climbs out of the shaft, he stands erect and angry, awaiting Kruger's reaction before he even twitches. In a brief battle, Slade almost toys with the pathetic opponent before he kicks his worthless carcass down the shaft, this time all the way down to his thumping death.

And the final confrontation between Tarzan and Slade occurs atop a rocky cliff, overlooking magnificent waterfalls, with Slade able to ensnare the jungle man in his wire noose (held tight at the end of a wooden pole) that he uses to strangle Tarzan from a safe distance. Of course in the well-choreographed fight to the death, Tarzan eventually survives, bellowing out his jungle cry atop the rocky mountain. Angie, now free and back on the river returning to safety, is watched from the distance by Tarzan, who continues his trek back home, having won the domination of his world and purging nature's domain of man-made evil. In this production, the focus is rightfully always on Gordon Scott's Tarzan, and the former jungle innocent becomes a symbol of unfettered strength and power, proving that the jungle cannot support two kings.

Such a crisp and energetic movie, and one populated with well-acted and developed characters, becomes the standard in the newly restructured Sy Weintraub-Gordon Scott Tarzan series. This B production, acted and directed to near perfection, became one of the pivotal action adventure movies of its time. For me, Tarzan movies do not get any better than *Tarzan's Greatest Adventure*. While the movie is almost non-stop action, it is focused equally on complex and psychologically challenged characters.

Finally, in 1960, at Gordon Scott's physical and the series' artistic peak, Scott starred in one final Tarzan adventure, *Tarzan the Magnificent*, a movie that many believe ranks right up there with *Tarzan's Greatest Adventure*. Producer Sy Weintraub returned, but this time the director was Robert Day (who co-wrote the screenplay), the man who directed *First Man Into Space*, many subsequent Tarzan entries and tons of British television including *Danger Man* and *The Avengers*. Continuing with adult themes and complex character

Tarzan and masterful villain Anthony Quayle fight for supremacy of the jungle in *Tarzan's Greatest Adventure*.

interaction, *Tarzan the Magnificent* presented the most literate Gordon Scott performance yet. In this production Scott has a solid command of the language and speaks in well-formulated sentences. Like the last film, Tarzan is armed with his bow and arrow and his prowess with the weapon saves the day in several sequences. Scott, still buffed, has a more natural physique with a less pronounced barrow chest, one that protruded so dramatically in the earlier MGM entries. So his better command of the language and a more toned-down physique make him a more natural hero, one dedicated to peace but not adverse to violence if violence becomes necessary.

As is always true with the better Scott entries, the supporting cast is outstanding with both Americans and Continental types appearing in well-written roles. Most outstanding is chief villain Coy Banton, played by American TV hero/Western star Jock Mahoney (*Yancy Derringer*). Mahoney's Coy Banton is a cool operator, always remaining calm and confident, a sneer or "I-just-outsmarted-you" smile on his lips. Mahoney becomes a formidable adversary to Tarzan, and their hand-to-hand combat at the end (with Mahoney stripped to the waist) is worthy of similar fistfights from any of the soon-to-emerge James Bond series. Father Abel Banton, played by an intense John Carradine, commands the crime family. He is the type of tough-love father who snaps his fingers and his evil brood jumps to his wishes. His children are all bastard murderers, seemingly incapable of following orders of any kind. On the other side of the cast, those characters that travel with and work for Tarzan's cause, some marginally, are Ames (an energetic Lionel Jeffries, soon to star

in *First Men in the Moon*) and his unhappy wife Fay (Betta St. John, who played Diana in *Tarzan and the Lost Safari*), Laurie (Alexandra Stewart) and Tate (Earl Cameron).

The action occurs in Kenya, Africa where a murderous family of robbers, the Banton gang, use their Jeep to sneak attack settlement stores and banks, always using automatic weapons to wipe out any opposition. And they seldom leave any survivors. Coy Banton, the most ruthless gang member, has a $5,000 ransom offered for his capture. When one policeman sneaks up to the jungle camp where the outlaws hide out, the policeman overtakes Coy in the middle of the night. The rest of the family are very upset and vow, rather calmly, to get him back. As the policeman and Coy travel by canoe down the river, an ambush awaits, when Coy flips the boat over to crreate a diversion. Then hidden members of the family come out blazing and rip rounds of hot metal into the defenseless lawman. However, the ambush has another element of surprise. Also hidden in the trees, Tarzan fires his bow and arrow, shooting down from high above, and kills one of the Banton siblings and wounds another. Tarzan gets the drop on Coy and subdues the murderer, swearing he will deliver Coy to the police and make sure the slain policeman's family receives the reward.

When Tarzan returns to the settlement hospital, everyone is afraid to house the captured Coy, fearing repercussion from his violent family. Only one elder African native allows Tarzan to hide the man in his hut. Tarzan plans to wait for the boat that will carry them down the river to the police drop-off point, but the Banton gang, headed by wizened Abel, attacks the boat and sets it ablaze, leaving it a flaming cinder. The passengers on board are left on the shore to fend for themselves. This means that Tarzan will have to transport Coy on foot through the jungle hills and valleys, and most importantly, the swamp.

Tarzan's traveling companion, the elderly Brit Ames, talks the big talk about only those who are number one succeed and number twos are failures, but when push comes to shove, Ames reveals himself to be a coward, and his sulking wife realizes this. She is seduced almost psychologically by the macho Coy Banton and starts to undermine Tarzan's plans and works convincingly for Coy's eventual escape. Tarzan sets elaborate tracks to make it appear the party is traveling over the jungle mountains, tricking Banton's party into searching for them in the wrong locale, when in fact they are shortcutting it through the deadly quicksand-laden swamp. Coy and Fay work together to drop one of her fancy handkerchiefs on the ground to alert Abel and the boys that Tarzan's entourage is headed through the swamps, not the mountains. Later in the film, when a lion devours Fay, no one is very sad, not even her husband Ames. The remainder of the movie is a cat-and-mouse chase through the jungle, with Banton's gang hoping to free Coy before he is turned over to the authorities.

Tarzan The Magnificent has several spectacular sequences—the Banton attack on the riverboat, the cold-blooded execution of the boat's pilot and the resulting boat burning are riveting. Another gripping moment is when Baton's gang arrives at the settlement searching for Coy, Tarzan hiding from the murderers and holding a knife at Coy's throat. A similar sequence occurs in the swamp, near the quicksand, as Tarzan and Coy are submerged in the muck, a knife again held at Coy's throat, and even when the Banton crew passes by Tarzan, it takes all of Tarzan's strength to get both Coy and himself free of the quicksand. The ambush sequence where the Bantons kill the policeman transporting Coy down the river is another shocker. And the final battle to the death, with Coy and Tarzan atop a rocky bluff, provides another scenic backdrop for the ultimate battle. In the violent altercation, Coy slips on brass knuckles to knock Tarzan unconscious, but the bloodied ape man revives and wins the battle, delivering the fiend to the police to stand trail for murder and collect the reward to deliver to the slain man's family.

In spite of such strengths and Jock Mahoney's inspired, underplayed performance, the film lacks the intense simplicity of the

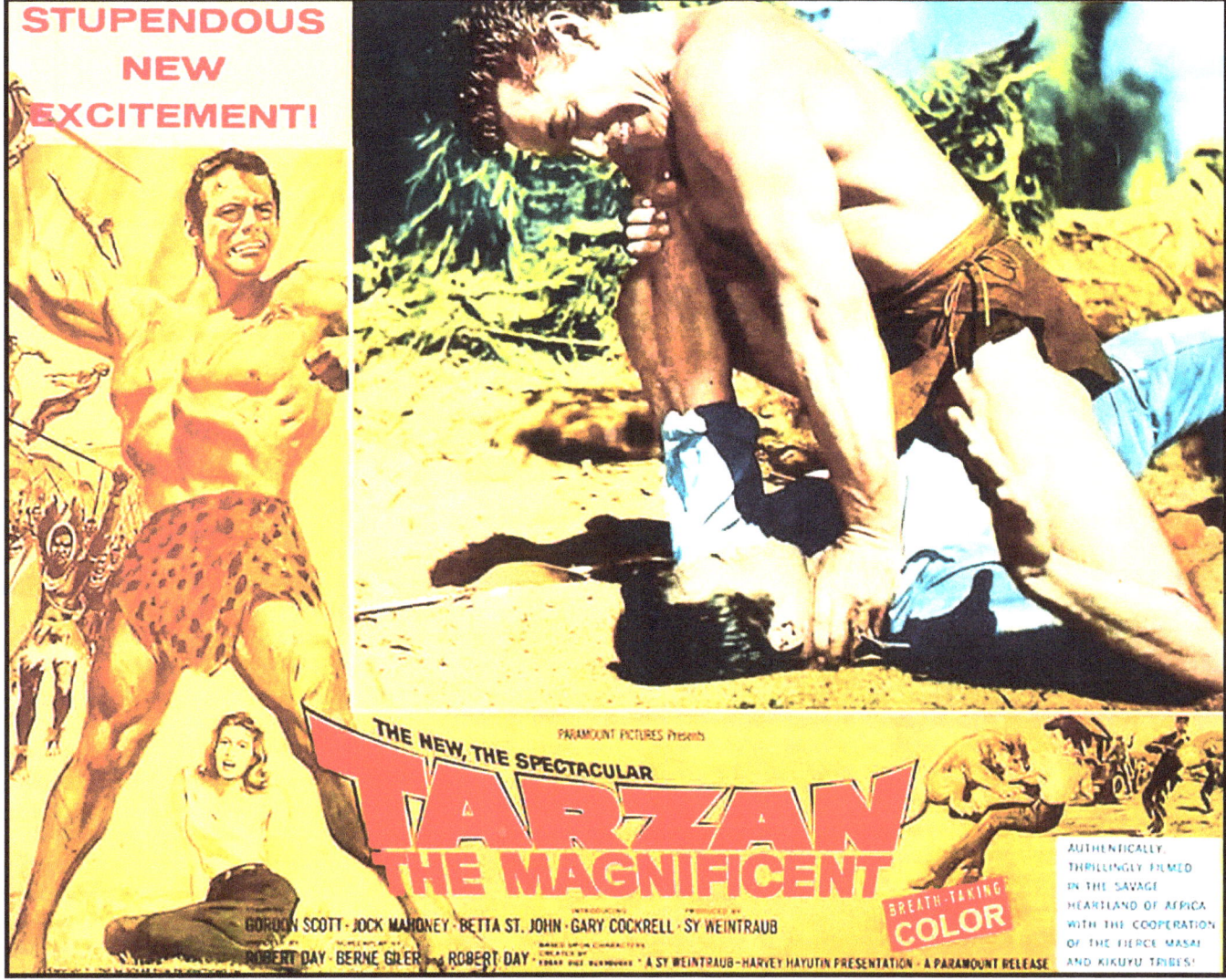

earlier *Tarzan's Greatest Adventure*, so I would rate this film overall a hair lower. Mind you, only a hair. Both films are superior action adventure movies and both have their particularly strong aspects, but once in a while my attention wanes while watching *Tarzan the Magnificent*, something that never occurred while watching *Tarzan' Greatest Adventure*. Even though Jock Mahoney and John Carradine are superb villains, they are external in that their inner motivations are never made clear. Basically, they are one-dimensional. However, Niall MacGinnis and Anthony Quayle, the villains of *Tarzan's Greatest Adventure*, are far less stereotyped and their characters are richly developed to establish their motivations. In other words, MacGinnis and Quayle are more fully developed villains and thus they imbue the film with added interest.

Besides the outstanding battle at the end of *Tarzan the Magnificent* (in many ways a mirror image of the battle at the end of *Tarzan's Greatest Adventure*), another major dramatic aspect of the film is the understated simmering passion that erupts between Coy and Fay, who falls under his sexual spell, with never a word being spoken. However, when the two escape and roam the African plains, Fay becomes tired and wishes to stop to rest. Coy gives her a passionate kiss and keeps on walking, abandoning the women he only used to gain his freedom, not actually caring for Fay one bit (she steals a key worn around Tarzan's neck, while he sleeps, to uncuff Coy, allowing both of them to make their escape). This relationship is presented visually, very subtly, perhaps becoming director Robert Day's finest moment in the film. However, Gordon Scott's Tarzan is always front and center and his jungle hero dominates and carries the production. And Gordon Scott has never been better.

Surprisingly, Gordon Scott's contract was not picked up, as producer Sy Weintraub was looking for a different style/new direction Tarzan, so the subsequent Tarzan entries, produced once again by Weintraub, starred former villain Jock Mahoney as Tarzan. Mahoney, lacking the "Mr. Universe" physique that Gordon Scott boasted, was more similar in appearance to Lex Barker. And Mahoney's Tarzan was more intellectual, using his brain over his brawn (Mahoney was, after all, six years older than Gordon Scott, and his first Tarzan movie appeared in 1962, two years after *Tarzan the Magnificent*). While Mahoney was perhaps the superior actor, his Tarzan was physically lackluster when compared to Gordon Scott, whose physical presence allowed him to tower over and own the role. Weintraub turned the franchise into little more than a Technicolor travelogue of exotic locations. Mahoney's venture into the Tarzan franchise was the beginning of the end, for no Tarzan movie produced after *Tarzan the Magnificent* quite dominated the box-office, gained kudos from the critics or garnered the emotional appeal of Gordon Scott. For many, Gordon Scott is remembered as the greatest screen Tarzan of all time. And Scott's final two Tarzan movies make that artistic statement quite convincingly.

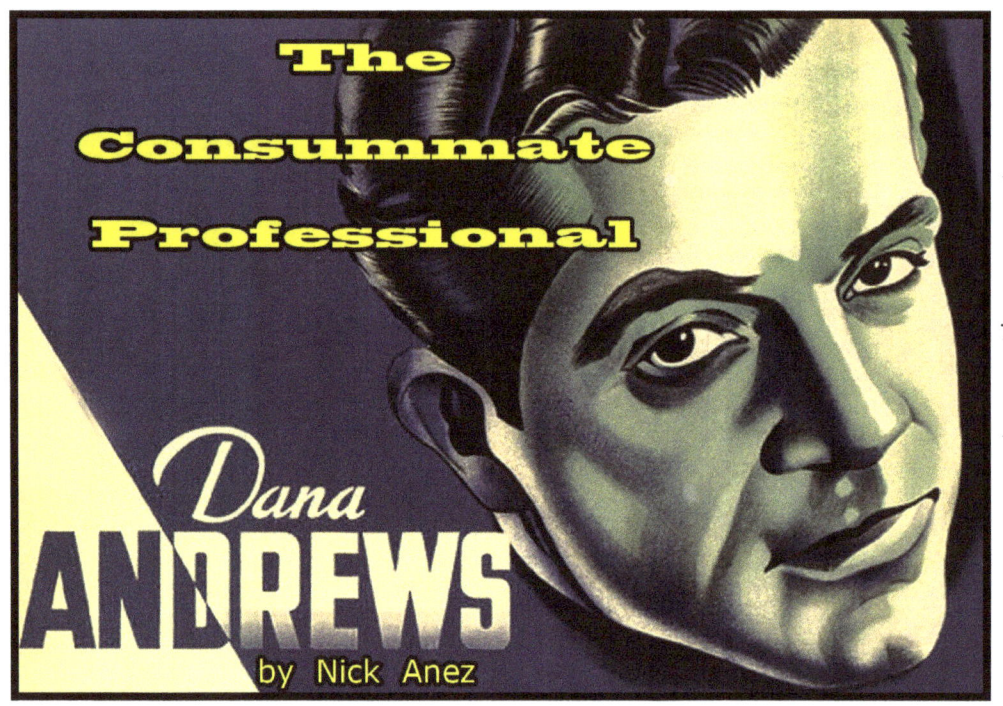

The Consummate Professional
Dana ANDREWS
by Nick Anez

The history of Hollywood is filled with actors that never received due appreciation for their talents. Perhaps these actors gave only passable performances when that was all the studio system required, placing them in mediocre projects. However, when called upon to add more depth and characterization, these actors often excelled with memorable portrayals. Nevertheless, they have rarely been given the recognition they deserve. An ideal example of this neglect is Dana Andrews.

Throughout his four-decade career, Dana Andrews appeared in over 75 movies. He began in supporting roles in the early 1940s and ended his career in supporting roles in the late 1980s. He worked with some of the most renowned directors in Hollywood, including Otto Preminger (5 movies), Lewis Milestone (4 movies), Jacques Tourneur (3 movies), William Wyler (2 movies), Fritz Lang (2 movies), William Wellman (2 movies), Elia Kazan (2 movies), Jean Renoir and John Ford (one movie each). From 1943 to 1950, he starred in his best films and provided several outstanding performances. But he never received an Academy Award nomination, much less winning an award.

Dana Andrews was born in 1909 in Covington County, Mississippi. He was the son of a Baptist minister, one of nine children. His family moved to Huntsville, Texas (where his younger brother, actor Steve Forrest, was born). He attended Sam Houston State Teachers College and studied business administration. After working as a bookkeeper, he hitchhiked to California in 1931 to pursue a career as a singer. He worked as a laborer, fruit picker, ditch digger and various other jobs while trying to break into the movies. His employer at a gas station in Van Nuys, believing in his talent, invested in him allowing Andrews to study music and join the Pasadena Community Playhouse, where he appeared in numerous plays during the 1930s. After several years, Andrews finally got his big break when producer Samuel Goldwyn signed him to a contract. When Goldwyn sold half of his contract to 20th Century Fox, he was in the enviable position of being legally bound to both a major studio and a major independent producer.

Andrews' first screen appearance was in a modest Fox programmer called *Lucky Cisco Kid* in 1940. His first film for Goldwyn was *The Westerner*, directed by William Wyler in 1940, which starred Gary Cooper. In 1941, Fox provided him with roles in *Belle Starr* and John Ford's *Tobacco Road*. These two films starred Gene Tierney, but Andrews was not the male lead in either film. His billing was noticeably smaller in size than that of Tierney, with whom he would so memorably co-star in the future. The studio gave him a larger role in Jean Renoir's first American feature, *Swamp Water*. In this movie his name was fourth (after Walter Brennan, Walter Huston

Gene Tierney and Dana Andrews in *Belle Starr*

Walter Brennan and Dana Andrews in *Swamp Water*

The film begins as two cowboys, Gil Carter and Art Croft, ride into town just as news arrives of the killing of a local rancher by cattle rustlers. Since the sheriff is out of town, a mob of vigilantes rides off in pursuit of the killers. Heading the group is a former Confederate officer, Major Tetley, who forces his peaceable son to accompany them. Gil and Art also join to avoid becoming suspects. The posse comes upon a campfire and the three men—Martin, Martinez and Harvey—who they believe to be the killers. It quickly becomes apparent that most of the members of the posse are not interested in determining the truth. Vigilante law is swift and brutal and soon revealed to be legalized murder. The lynchers return to town to face legal and moral justice for their crime.

The movie received an Academy Award nomination for Best Picture of the Year. It has been occasionally criticized for its obvious studio sets. However, Wellman took advantage of his limited budget and utilized artificial trees and synthetic lighting to create an environment that is deliberately unreal, as though reflecting the unreasoning madness of the mob. The reading of Martin's letter, which was not in the novel, has also been the subject of criticism, due to its preachy tone. Some critics feel that a man about to die wouldn't be so literary. But the mood of the entire movie is so somber that the reading of the letter seems to fit within the story.

and Anne Baxter), but it was the first time he was billed above the title. In 1942, Fox gave Andrews his first starring role in a wartime B movie, *Berlin Correspondent*, which proved to be a good showcase for the rising star.

The year 1943 proved to be an important one for Dana Andrews. He supported Tyrone Power and Anne Baxter in Fox's *Crash Dive*, which showed that he could hold his own with the studio's biggest stars. He was also given a lead role in Goldwyn's *The North Star*, which was his first of three films for director Lewis Milestone. (After World War II, when Russia was no longer an ally of the United States, the pro-Soviet film was re-edited with its title changed to *Armored Attack*.)

It was also in 1943 that Andrews delivered his first truly great performance in the Fox production of *The Ox-Bow Incident*. Based upon the novel by Walter Van Tilburg Clark and directed by William Wellman, the movie remains harrowing today in its depiction of mob violence in the Old West. Andrews was billed second and in smaller letters than the star of the movie, Henry Fonda, and his role is a supporting one. However, it is his performance that stands out among the fine cast.

Dana Andrews (left), Anthony Quinn (center) and Frank Conroy as Major Tetley (right) from *The Ox-Bow Incident*

Henry Fonda gets the jump on Dana Andrews from *The Ox-Bow Incident*.

Fonda and Henry Morgan are believable as decent cowboys with Fonda's character burdened by his own flaws. Frank Conroy as Major Tetley and Jane Darwell as Ma Grier stand out among the posse members. As the accused victims of mob justice, Anthony Quinn captures the inherent fatalism of Martinez while Francis Ford is particularly impressive as the befuddled old man who just wants to live.

However, it is the performance of Dana Andrews as Donald Martin that stands out. He makes his character a tragic victim through his immersion in the role. It is a heartrending portrayal, filled with emotional resonance. He registers shock, fear, despair and eventually acceptance convincingly as his character gradually realizes the hopelessness of his situation. When he breaks down, his tears are not for himself but for his wife and children. The scene in which he writes his letter to his wife is especially memorable. Knowing that all of his efforts to appeal to the decency of the vigilantes have failed, he tries to control his emotions as he struggles for the correct words to make his wife understand why he will never see her again. As the members of the mob laugh and drink nearby, his feelings of misery and fury are reflected in his expression and tone. It is bewildering that Dana Andrews did not receive an Oscar nomination for his extremely sensitive performance.

Nominated that year in the Best Supporting Actor category were Charles Bickford for *The Song of Bernadette*, Charles Coburn

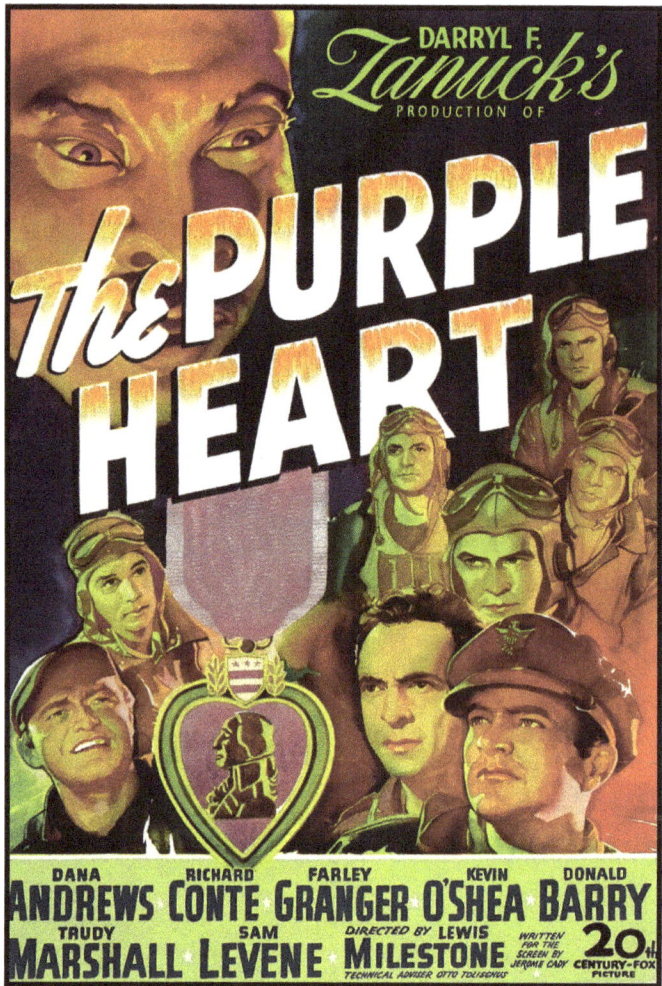

for *The More the Merrier*, J. Carrol Naish for *Sahara*, Claude Rains for *Casablanca* and Akim Tamiroff for *For Whom the Bell Tolls*. These are all good performances but, except for Naish's portrayal of an Italian prisoner in the World War II drama, none of these performances is exceptional, including that of Coburn, who won. But they were all in commercially successful movies while *The Ox-Bow Incident*, though a critical success, did not fare too well at the box office. This perhaps may explain the lack of a nomination for Andrews. But his equally superb performances in box-office hits in the future would be similarly ignored.

The Ox-Bow Incident made Dana Andrews a star. After one more supporting role in Goldwyn's Danny Kaye vehicle *Up in Arms* (1944), he received starring billing in movies for the next 15 years. And it was also in 1944 that he gave his next two award-worthy performances. Actually, Andrews had four movies released in 1944. In addition to the Kaye musical, he co-starred with Don Ameche in *A Wing and a Prayer*, headed an ensemble cast in *The Purple Heart* and topped off the year with *Laura*. Not many actors could be cast so convincingly in such widely divergent roles within the same year, but Andrews pulled it off with professional ease.

Fox released *The Purple Heart*, directed by Lewis Milestone, in February, while the country was still in the midst of WW II. The movie, out of necessity filled with speculation, is based upon the true story of eight-captured airman who took part in Lt. Col. Jimmy Doolittle's bombing raid over Tokyo. The men were tried by the Japanese in a civilian court, which had no legal jurisdiction over military personnel, and sentenced to death. The exact details of the trial and aftermath were not known at the time of the movie's production and it was believed that all of the men had been executed. After the war, it was discovered that three men had been executed and one died in captivity. The remaining four were liberated at the end of the war.

The movie begins in a Japanese courtroom where eight American airmen are falsely charged with targeting civilian and non-military installations. The lead officer is Captain Harvey Ross. In charge of the prosecution is General Mitsubi, who is determined to force the men to confess that their plane was launched from an aircraft carrier and not from the Aleutians as they claimed. (Medium bombers, such as B-25s, had never before been launched from a carrier and it was imperative for the Japanese to learn if this had actually occurred.) The eight men refuse to cooperate and are subjected to torture, but no one breaks, even though the men suffer horribly. Eventually, Mitsubi promises Ross that if they cooperate their lives will be spared. However, the men maintain their loyalty, causing Mitsubi to commit suicide. But it also leads to a sentence of death for the men.

Dana Andrews heads the cast as Captain Ross. All of the actors who portray the prisoners deliver first-rate performances, with Richard Conte and Farley Granger particularly impressive. However, it is Andrews who stands out, not only because of his leadership role, but because he has the meatiest scene at the end of the movie. He delivers a patriotic speech to the courtroom with just the right amount of anger, fervor and righteousness. It is not surprising that this portrayal cemented Andrews as a major star.

The Purple Heart is admittedly propaganda and was especially emotional for wartime audiences. However, the U.S. government objected to the production and decreed that no atrocities by the Japanese could be depicted. Fox production chief Darryl F. Zanuck, who had written the original story under the name of Melville Crossman, was nevertheless determined to make the movie and filmed it on closed sets to avoid censorship or intervention by the War Department. While the movie was being filmed, there was a distinct possibility that it would not be released. However, in January 1944, the War Department issued a statement detailing the atrocities that had been committed upon American prisoners following the defeats of Bataan and Corregidor. In view of this, the ban was lifted and the film was released. While the movie was in theaters, some personnel in the War Department continued to object to the content of the movie due to fears that the depicted scenes might have a detrimental effect upon recruitment.

The very political film contains clichés familiar to other wartime movies. The men symbolize the usual cross-section of American society, with many diverse nationalities all represented. And also the Japanese are portrayed as ruthless brutes. Due to this depiction, the movie today is considered in some circles to be racist. Unfortunately, the atrocities to which the men were subjected were not atypical. Allied prisoners were subjected to inhumane treatment by Japanese soldiers and, according to later statistics, almost 50% died in captivity from lack of medical treatment, torture, starvation and execution. What happened to the men in this film happened to thousands of allied prisoners and no amount of revisionist history by Clint Eastwood can change that fact. This is not to say that resentments should still be held over 60 years later. But history shouldn't be changed to suit political correctness, as exemplified by Eastwood's *Letters from Iwo Jima* (2006). And it should be remembered that it is the Japanese military, not the Japanese people, who are depicted so negatively.

As evident from reports after the war, it was clear that the trial was rigged with manufactured evidence and that the guilty verdict was ordained from the beginning. The true story of the trial of the eight crewmen and the tortures to which they were subjected can be found in the book, *Four Came Home* by Carroll V. Glines (Van Nostrand Reinhold; 1966). As General Doolittle wrote in his introduction to the book, "The purpose is not to open old wounds or to condemn the Japanese. Rather, it is told so that we will all remember what evils an uncontrolled militaristic government can bring to its people."

Andrews provided another memorable role the same year in Otto Preminger's *Laura*, which Fox released in October. In this movie, his third with Gene Tierney, he is no longer a supporting star but

Emphasizing the film noir elements with the high contrast lighting, Dana Andrews confronts Gene Tierney in *Laura*.

Detective McPherson (Andrews) finds himself staring down the rifle of Shelby Carpenter (Vincent Price) in *Laura*.

a co-star with equal billing. He plays Detective Mark McPherson, who is in charge of the investigation into the apparent murder of Laura Hunt. The body of a woman, her face torn apart by a shotgun blast, is discovered in Laura's apartment. Mark's investigation brings him into contact with several people who were closest to Laura. Waldo Lydecker, an acerbic columnist and radio personality, made her a success in her career as an advertising executive and introduced her into his world of uptown society. Shelby Carpenter, a smooth-talking gigolo, was engaged to Laura but was also involved with two other women, including Ann Treadwell, who is as possessive of Shelby as Waldo was of Laura. These people inhabit a different world than Mark's and consider him to be below their social status. But Mark can see through their pseudo-sophistication and considers them all possible suspects.

Initially, the stoiac Mark seems to be devoid of any outward emotion and is interested only in solving the murder. Almost against his will, he gradually becomes obsessed with Laura. He stares at her portrait, reads her diary, inhales her perfume and finds himself attracted to the image he develops of her. One evening, Mark stares at Laura's portrait as he drinks himself into slumber. When he awakens he finds Laura Hunt very much alive. It seems that the woman who was killed was Shelby's former girlfriend who was mistaken by the killer for Laura. Laura's re-emergence among the living re-ignites all of the passions that had been suspended with her supposed death. Mark not only has to uncover the killer but realizes that he is now personally involved because he is in love with Laura. But does he love Laura or the fantasy woman he imagined her to be? All of these emotions build to an explosive climax.

A summary of the movie's plot cannot begin to encompass the film's stylishness and sophistication or its witty and chic dialogue. Director Preminger, who received an Oscar nomination for this film, initially uses his camera to create an aura of mystery about Laura, as though he is slowly creating a fantasy image just as Waldo had done and Mark slowly begins to do. Simultaneously with the romantic obsession developed by the outsider-cop, the corruption and decadence of the upper class is gradually exposed.

Clifton Webb as Waldo Lydecker received most of the critical praise (as well as an Oscar nominating as Best Supporting Actor). He creates a marvelous portrait of a supercilious and pompous man who sincerely believes that his self-absorption is fully justified. This was Webb's breakthrough role in the movies. A former professional ballroom dancer and star of the Broadway and London stage, he had appeared in a few silent movies during the 1920s but remained off the screen for almost two decades until Preminger tapped him to play Lydecker. Vincent Price and Judith Anderson also received acclaim for their portrayals of Shelby and Ann. Gene Tierney, in the title role, was celebrated for her ability to convey Laura's mystery and charisma. Some critics accused her of playing the role in a distant manner, not realizing that this distance was deliberate and designed to enhance her mystery, at least until she is brought down to earth by her love for Mark.

As Mark McPherson, Dana Andrews perfectly conveys the qualities of a film noir protagonist. He once again gives a performance that was taken for granted, particularly since it is a quieter portrayal than all of his co-stars. His troubled eyes and quietly crafty voice create an image that is unromantic on the surface yet still suggestive of sensitivity. In this movie, he displays a deceptively commanding

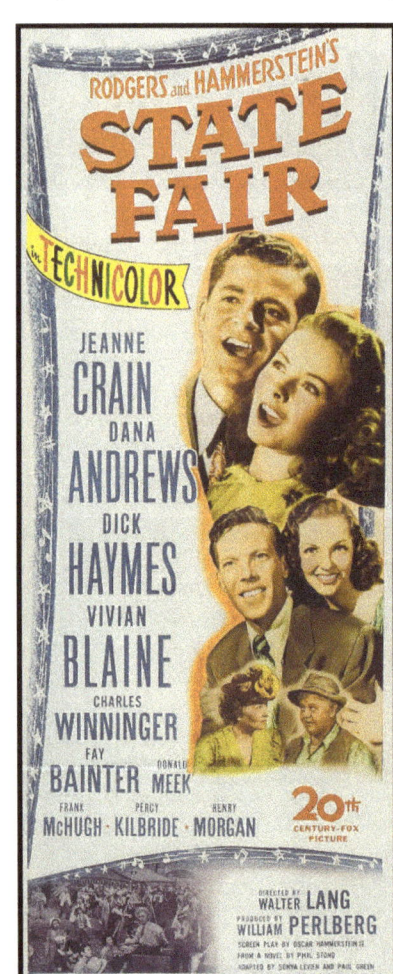

Dana Andrews, the cad, marries lovely Alice Faye for her money, in *Fallen Angel*.

This is the story of an American infantry platoon that takes a "walk in the sun" in the Italian countryside on its way to complete a mission that is merely a small part of the worldwide conflagration surrounding them. The movie begins with the landing of the platoon on the beaches of Salerno. Almost immediately, the platoon is crippled by the deaths of the ranking officers which leaves Sergeant Porter in charge. The platoon's mission is to capture a farmhouse in the countryside that is occupied by German forces. However, the responsibility eventually proves to be too much for Porter, who suffers a mental breakdown. Leadership then falls to Sergeant Bill Tyne who doesn't want it any more than Porter did, but he accepts it because there is no alternative. Somehow, Tyne knows that he must conquer his fears and insecurities and complete the mission.

On their way to the farmhouse, the men of the platoon engage in small talk as they try to stay alive and keep fear from overtaking them. The movie makes clear, as the novel does, that war is often a period of waiting. In between the spurts of violence, as they await the next threat to their lives, they try to keep the possibility of death from entering their minds. These men don't dwell on their anxieties or fears but just accept them and do their best to contain them. During the quiet scenes of conversation, they don't talk about the war. They talk about their personal desires and wishes. It is as though the war is secondary to them. Their personal memories are uppermost in their minds and create an armor against the violence of the war.

The emotional impact of the story builds steadily as the platoon gets increasingly closer to its objective. As Private Rivera repeatedly says, "Nobody dies." The men hope that this will be true even though they know that it won't be. Death does occur, periodically and suddenly, whether from aircraft overhead, armored tanks on the ground or machine guns in the farmhouse. Action is swift and violent in this film, but no blood and gore is actually shown. When the lieutenant has half his face blown off at the beginning of the movie, it does not have to be graphically depicted for the horror to register. The movie depicts death in an almost discreet manner and underplaying is what makes each death so poignant. Because each of the men has been carefully fleshed out through bits and pieces of dialogue, viewers have gotten to know them. As a result, their deaths

screen presence, whose expressions, particularly his reactions to the affectations of his suspects, convey more than many actors do with a dozen lines of dialogue. His delivery of lines is equally rewarding. When he says, "A doll in Washington Heights got a fox fur out of me once," or "Dames are always pulling a switch on you," his lines are delivered with just the right amount of intonation and sarcasm, yet with just an implication of veiled vulnerability. At the same time, Mark's gradual infatuation with a dead woman suggests something unhealthy. The fantasy that he creates in his mind of Laura makes him to some degree the mirror image of Lydecker. His expression as he stares up at the portrait of Laura is one of the great images of romantic obsession. This is a terrific performance from Andrews that is essential to the film's durability. *Laura* was a huge commercial success and certified Andrews as a major star.

Not many actors could play a hard-edged detective and then follow it with an equally convincing lead in a musical, but Dana Andrews did just that. In 1945, Andrews starred in the Fox production of Rodgers and Hammerstein's *State Fair*. It is interesting that, although he was an excellent singer, he kept this talent a secret because he did not want to be typed as a musical star. As a result, his voice was dubbed when he was required to sing. Also that year, Andrews reunited with Otto Preminger for another Fox mystery-noir, *Fallen Angel*. He plays a shady opportunist who marries a woman for deceitful reasons. Once again, he is saved by the love of a woman, but his character is totally the opposite of Mark McPherson. The movie was not the critical or financial success that *Laura* was, but it did prove that Andrews could play a cad as convincingly as a hero.

For Dana's third movie of the year, Lewis Milestone personally requested the actor's services from Samuel Goldwyn for his independent production of *A Walk in the Sun*, based upon the novel of the same name by Harry Brown. The movie is an incisive character study of men in war which totally avoids the stereotypes of so many other war movies. In concentrating on a single platoon and its relatively minor mission, the movie makes a universal statement about war. Unlike *The Purple Heart*, there are no patriotic speeches and no melodramatic heroics. It is a film that is both realistic and artistic. It is a film filled with irony, from its title to the fact that men who long to be home with their families are being asked to die for an objective that seems to have little value.

Dana Andrews plays Sgt. Bill Tyne, creating a performance of restrain and force in *A Walk in the Sun*.

are shattering. And when the final battle for the farmhouse takes place, the savagery of war is depicted with horrifying immediacy.

As Sergeant Bill Tyne, Dana Andrews provides a forceful yet restrained portrayal and it is this moderation that gives his character credibility. However, Andrews is just one member of a fine ensemble cast, all of whom perform with equal skill. Richard Conte, Lloyd Bridges and John Ireland make notable impressions and would reach various levels of stardom in the future. Also standing out is Herbert Rudley as Sergeant Porter, a man who finds refuge from the war by retreating within his own broken mind.

Incidentally, there is a ballad entitled "It Was Just a Little Walk in the Sun" that is heard throughout the movie. After introducing each of the men of the platoon, the film's narrator says, "Here is a song about them. Listen." It may seem odd for a war movie to have a theme song that periodically provides commentary upon the action (as numerous Westerns would do the following decade), but the tune and lyrics fit in perfectly with the stylized and occasionally poetic dialogue of the movie.

A Walk in the Sun was beset with problems during filming. Since Allied Artists was to release this independent production, original producer Samuel Bronston borrowed money to finance the film. When the lending corporations discovered that the movie could not be completed on the promised budget, they took over the production. Here the rights were transferred to a corporation co-owned by Lewis Milestone and the movie was completed. During post-production, Darryl F. Zanuck purchased distribution rights to the movie and released it through 20th Century Fox.

Robert Rossen's screenplay is a very faithful adaptation of the novel, with much of the dialogue taken verbatim. Russell Harlan's striking cinematography with its shadings of light and darkness is also noteworthy. But *A Walk in the Sun* did not receive any Academy Award nominations and was not a notable financial success. Nevertheless, it qualifies as the World War II equivalent of Milestone's 1930 World War I classic, *All Quiet on the Western Front*. The pacifism of the earlier film may be missing but the director's indictment of the horrors of war remains just as scathing.

In 1946, Dana's contracts with Fox and Goldwyn became non-exclusive, which allowed him to work at other studios. That year, he starred in two movies, the first titled *Canyon Passage*, which Universal released in July. This Western is one of those rare films in which everything works perfectly, from the ideal casting to the unsentimental script, from the fine direction to the dazzling photography. The movie is filled with credible characters and plausible relationships, as well as spine-tingling action scenes and suspenseful drama. The setting is an Oregon mining town in the middle of the 19th Century. The community is filed with miners, merchants, gamblers and thieves, as well as settlers who are clearing the surrounding land for farming. And there are the Indians who are slowly losing their homeland to the whites. This precarious situation has resulted in an uneasy truce. All it takes is one spark to set off an explosion.

Logan Stuart is a gung-ho freighter and businessman with hopes of building a commercial empire. He doesn't know that his partner, banker and compulsive gambler George Camrose, has started to embezzle money in order to pay off his debts. George is engaged to Lucy Overmire, while Logan is planning to marry Caroline Marsh, daughter of a settler. Logan also has a deadly enemy in Honey Bragg, a primitive thug who is accustomed to using brute force to get what he wants. Other characters include Hi Litton, a happy-go-lucky minstrel who has a habit of peering into windows, Ben Dance, a good-natured farmer who just wants to live with his family in peace and Johnny Steel, a young hothead who enjoys the power of vigilante justice in the absence of official law.

The violence begins with an attempted robbery which sets the tone for the movie, despite the tranquil scenes that follow. The

Dana Andrews, center, is surrounded by Brian Donlevy, Hoagy Carmichael and Lloyd Bridges, from *Canyon Passage*.

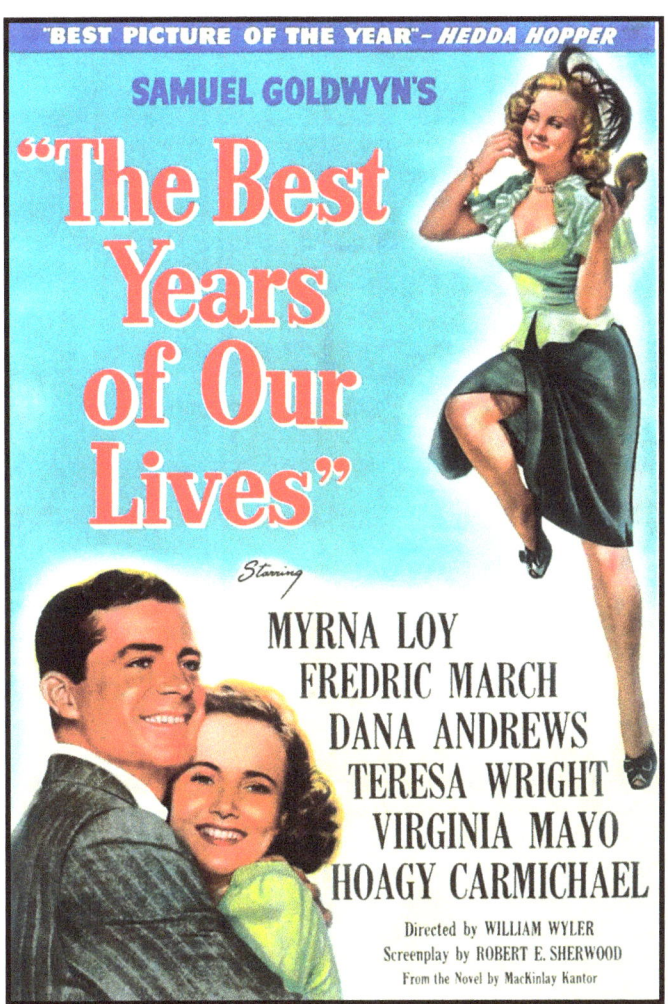

hostility between Logan and Bragg eventually leads to a brutal fight. These acts appear to be normal, almost expected occurrences within the frontier community. However, the violence escalates when George kills a miner who has demanded his gold. This leads to increasing friction between Logan and the townspeople, particularly after a kangaroo court finds George guilty and sentences him to death. Meanwhile, Bragg rapes and murders an Indian girl, which precipitates a rampage by the Indians. The conflict that follows is merciless and consumes many innocent lives, as well as guilty ones.

Jacques Tourneur directs *Canyon Passage* in a deceptively effortless manner that may appear to be simplistic on the surface but is actually the work of a skilled artist. This is the same director who had only recently created a classic horror movie, *Cat People*, and the following year would direct a classic film noir, *Out of the Past*. With this film, he displays an affinity for the American West that captures a time and place that is too often colored by myth and romance. His sense of action, conflict and sentiment combine to create a cohesive work that continues to delight upon repeated viewings. Tourneur had the benefit of a wonderful script by Ernest Pascal that vividly captures the rich assortment of characters, as well as the slightly archaic dialogue of Ernest Haycox's novel. The characters seem to actually live within a pioneer settlement with hopes and dreams that are realistic to a community that is slowly forming amidst the wilderness. Beneath the main storyline are several sub-plots, all of which co-exist and eventually converge.

In his first starring role in a frontier drama, Dana Andrews as Logan Stuart is as believable as a Western hero as he is in a soldier's uniform or in the rumpled clothing of a streetwise detective. He projects sturdiness, integrity and strength. It is a very masculine performance, in a traditional sense. He accepts Bragg's challenge without any deliberation, despite the larger man's advantage in size and his reputation for being a dirty fighter. He accepts Caroline's rejection gracefully and without any self-pity, displaying just the right amount of awareness to know she has made the correct decision for both of them.

Brain Donlevy as George initially evokes enough charm to make Lucy's attraction to him understandable, yet beneath the charm is a suggestion of weak moral character. Susan Hayward is very credible as Lucy, fully conveying her strength as well as her vulnerability. Ward Bond is particularly convincing as Bragg, displaying a malevolence that was opposed to his usual screen image. Patricia Roc as Caroline and Lloyd Bridges as Johnny turn in sturdy performances, but the entire cast contributes to the overall effectiveness of the movie. And, after watching this movie, it is impossible to not start singing "Ole Buttermilk Sky." But no one could sing it as beautifully as Hoagy Carmichael, whose understated performance as Hi Litton illustrates that he could fit into 1856 Oregon as comfortably as in a 1940 Martinique nightclub or in a post-War tavern in an American city—which leads to Dana Andrews' next and most famous movie.

In November, RKO released Samuel Goldwyn's justly celebrated masterpiece, *The Best Years of Our Lives*, which re-united Dana with William Wyler and provided him with the most challenging role of his career. The movie would win seven Academy Awards, including Best Picture, Best Actor and Best Supporting Actor. But Dana Andrews was not even nominated, despite the fact that his splendid performance is the centerpiece of the film.

The film concerns three returning war veterans who meet at a demobilization center and form a tentative friendship as they return to their home town of Boone City, located in an unspecified middle-American state. Though they are from different class levels, they share fear and anxiety over their ability to re-adjust to civilian life. Army Sergeant Al Stephenson returns to his wife Millie and two grown children, Peggie and Rob, in a rather luxurious apartment. Navy sailor Homer Parrish, who must adjust to the fact that he is a double amputee, having lost both hands, returns to his middle-class family. Air Force Captain Fred Derry visits his father and stepmother in a shanty to find that his wife Marie has moved into her own apartment. This is only the beginning of a story that celebrates the joys, happiness, hardships and humiliations experienced by the men who find that their lives and families have changed forever. The

movie interweaves the stories skillfully of the three men who remain in contact with one another as they experience various degrees of difficulty in their attempts to re-adjust to society.

Al has it relatively easy, having returned to a devoted family and his job as vice-president in charge of loans at the local bank. He has some initial problems re-establishing relationships with family members and with the bank president, who doesn't approve of his unorthodox policy of giving loans to veterans without collateral. But he at least has the comfort of a home, a family and a job. Homer Parrish has learned to cope without his hands but faces the reality of having to depend upon someone to take care of his needs for the rest of his life. He is also unsure whether his fiancée Wilma still wants to marry him out of love or pity. Having been a star football player in high school, he puts on a good show of acceptance of his fate but is still prone to bouts of depression and anger. Fred Derry has the most difficult time because it soon becomes clear that Marie has been unfaithful and that job prospects for a heroic fighter pilot are poor. To make matters worse, as Fred realizes that Marie doesn't love him, he and Peggy Stephenson are gradually attracted to one another, which does not please Al.

William Wyler, with compassion and integrity, brings to the screen the physical and psychological effects of war upon servicemen and their families. The screenplay by Robert E. Sherwood, based upon a novel in verse by MacKinlay Kantor, is beautifully assembled with every scene and line of dialogue meaningful and expository. The movie runs three hours but doesn't seem that long since not a single wasted moment exists, as the stories develop along their separate paths, mingling periodically, and then joining together for an extremely heartwarming finale.

Fredric March won the Best Actor award for his portrayal of Al Stephenson, and Harold Russell, an actual amputee, won two awards for his portrayal of Homer Parrish, one for Best Supporting Actor and another special award for giving hope to returning servicemen. March is excellent as Al but his role does not require the depth and range of emotion provided by Andrews. And he already won an Oscar for *Dr. Jekyll and Mr. Hyde* (1932). The injustice of the oversight of not nominating Dana is even more apparent when compared to the other nominees: Laurence Olivier for *Henry V*, Larry Parks for *The Jolson Story*, Gregory Peck for *The Yearling* and James Stewart for *It's a Wonderful Life*. Olivier was given an Academy Award for "outstanding achievement as actor, producer and director" for the Shakespearean drama, so he had nothing to complain about. Stewart is extremely good and deserved the nomination, but he also already had an Oscar for a rather standard performance in *The Philadelphia Story* (1940). Parks was rewarded for simply doing a good impersonation of Al Jolson and Peck's portrayal is pleasing if nothing special. Neither of these performances matched the impact of Andrews' portrayal of Fred Derry.

There are many examples of Andrews' superb skill in bringing Fred Derry to life. The scene in Peggy's bedroom in which he experiences what would later be called post-traumatic stress is frightening and gives a clear indication of the horrors he experienced. The next morning, his reaction to Peggy for not mentioning the incident is equally adroit in its subtlety. The expressions he displays as he receives one disappointment and rejection after another, both in his personal life and his employment, skillfully reflect increasing feelings of self-contempt and worthlessness. However, his most powerful scene is the one in which he climbs into a dismantled aircraft, sits in the pilot's seat and relives the trauma of his experiences. Slowly, almost imperceptibly, his expressions of fear, agony, terror and eventual relief reveal that he is finally able to expunge the gruesome memories from his mind. This scene alone should have won him a nomination.

Myrna Loy as Millie Stephenson and Theresa Wright as Peggy both give very touching performances. Virginia Mayo is properly bitchy as Marie and displays her true character when she rips off her false eyebrows in a fit of sulky anger. Hoagy Carmichael is again on hand to project his winsome personality as Butch, Ho-mer's uncle and the owner of the tavern in which the men regularly meet. *The Best Years of Our Lives* is a classic and contains a superlative Dana Andrews performance.

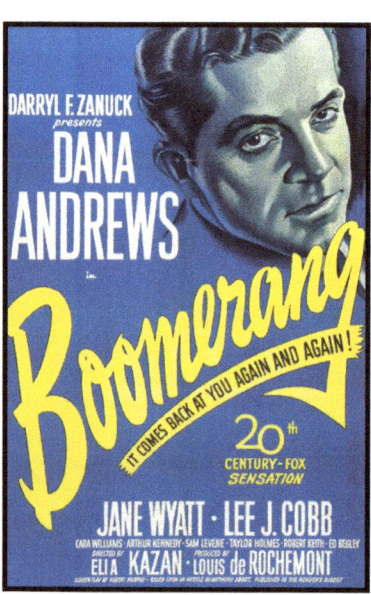

Andrew's next movie paired him with another major director, Elia Kazan, in Fox's 1947 production of *Boomerang!*. This is an excellent semi-documentary drama based upon an actual case. In a peaceful Connecticut town, a beloved minister is murdered and John Waldron, a vagrant, is charged with the crime. Though Waldron confesses after brutal interrogation, The State Attorney Henry

Dana Andrews, Joan Crawford and Henry Fonda star in *Daisy Kenyon*, the least of the Andrews-Preminger collaborations.

In 1948, Dana Andrews starred in four movies. But the year would prove to be a disappointing one for him since three of those movies were beneath his talents artistically, particularly in view of his recent achievements. In RKO's *Night Song*, he plays a blind pianist in a sudsy soap opera that has little of substance to recommend it. Fox's *Deep Waters* is an undistinguished drama about an orphan and a fisherman that did nothing for his career. Lewis Milestone, surprisingly, directed MGM's *No Minor Vices*. This dull domestic comedy is not the proper showcase for the talents of either the actor or director and is way below the level of their previous three films.

Andrews had a more fruitful reunion with William Wellman. *The Iron Curtain* was his second film for the director and his fourth with Gene Tierney. As another indication of his advanced marquee power, he is billed ahead of Tierney for the first time. This is a suspenseful cold war drama released by Fox and based upon a true story of Soviet espionage in Canada. Incidentally, a preview of the movie in New York was picketed by hundreds of Communists and sympathizers, as well as anti-Communists who supported the film. The publicity helped to make the movie a box-office hit.

Harvey, who is charged with prosecuting the crime, eventually believes in his innocence. Despite political pressure, Harvey risks his career and political future to prove that the evidence against Waldron is flawed. Andrews, who is billed alone above the title, delivers yet another fine performance as Harvey and is particularly mesmerizing in the courtroom climax in which he actually places his life in jeopardy. Also delivering fine performances are Arthur Kennedy as Waldron, Lee J. Cobb as the police chief and Ed Begley as a corrupt local politician.

Also in 1947, Fox released *Daisy Kenyon*. This was another Andrews-Preminger collaboration but is probably the least memorable of their films. Though there are again some noir elements to the film, the film is more of a romantic drama and a vehicle for star Joan Crawford. Henry Fonda also stars in this movie but this time Andrews is not only his full-fledged co-star but is billed above Fonda, certainly a clear indication of his enhanced status. In this movie, Andrews plays a man who is married to an abusive woman but loves his mistress, the woman of the title. He is quite good as a brilliant but self-centered lawyer who realizes too late that he can't have everything. The movie is interesting but doesn't quite hold together, though it was popular in its day.

Andrews starred in three movies in 1949. The best is a romantic melodrama for Samuel Goldwyn, *My Foolish Heart*. Even though he has top billing, his character dies long before the finale. It's really a woman's picture and a star vehicle for his co-star from *Canyon Passage*, Susan Hayward. The other two movies represent further setbacks in his career. *The Forbidden Street* (U.K. title: *Britannia Mews*) is an unmemorable historical drama for Fox in which he plays two roles, while *Sword in the Desert* is an unremarkable Universal programmer, the kind the studio turned out in droves.

At this point, Andrews' career was in danger of being in a downward slide. None of his recent movies illuminated his talent. However, Otto Preminger came to his rescue in 1950 and cast him and Gene Tierney in an excellent movie. *Where the Sidewalk Ends* provides him with one of his best roles as a morally compromised cop who is too quick with his fists. This Fox production doesn't take place in the posh settings of *Laura* but instead occurs in the dark and dirty streets of crime and corruption. It is tough, brutal and inflexible in its depiction of a man trapped hopelessly by his past and uncontrollable impulses.

Andrews plays Sergeant Mark Dixon, a cop with a history of brutality, who is given a warning by Lieutenant Thomas to go by

Dana Andrews appears with Gene Tierney for the fourth time in *The Iron Curtain*.

the book or risk losing his job. Dixon doesn't hesitate to express his hatred for criminals, due in part to the fact that his father was one. He has a particular vendetta against Tommy Scalise, a local crime boss and former associate of his father. When a stranger is killed during a crap game operated by Scalise, Dixon's investigation leads him to Ken Paine, a war hero who had fought with the murder victim. During his interrogation of Paine, Dixon loses his temper and accidentally kills him. Dixon covers up the crime but remains in charge of the investigation. He eventually learns that Paine had an estranged wife, Morgan Taylor, to whom he is attracted. But when circumstantial evidence incriminates Morgan's father, Dixon tries to direct evidence toward Scalise. As Dixon realizes little by little that there is no way out of the hole he has dug for himself, the film builds to a climax.

Andrews' three previous films with Preminger all contain noir elements to varying degrees (as does *Whirlpool*, which Preminger had directed with Tierney in 1949) and therefore fit within the genre. However, *Where the Sidewalk Ends* is more representative of genuine film noir. The movie encapsulates all of the qualities of noir, from its setting to its characters, from its entrapped protagonist to its atmosphere of hopelessness, from the oppressiveness of the interiors

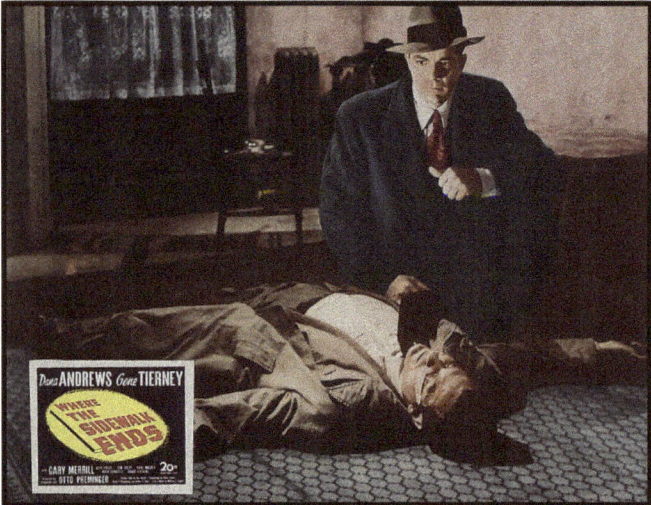

Over zealous cop Mark Dixon (Dana Andrews) stands over the body of Ken Paine, the man he accidentally killed.

to the rain-drenched streets. The tone is grim and downbeat as Mark's plight becomes increasingly desperate. The mood conveys a world of danger and despair, thanks not only to Preminger's assured direction but also to the razor-sharp script by Ben Hecht and terrific cinematography by Joseph La Shelle (who had functioned in the same capacity for *Laura* and *Fallen Angel*.)

Unlike *Laura* in which Mark McPherson is one of several characters vying for attention, Mark Dixon is the main focus of *Where the Sidewalk Ends*. His journey from hatred and corruption to love and redemption propels the movie. Dixon is not a successful cop, unlike Lt. Thomas who has risen from the ranks by obeying the book. Dixon sees himself as a failure, both in his profession and in his personal life. The contempt he feels for Scalise and his father is extended toward himself, because he suspects that deep down he is no better than either of them. When he inadvertently causes the death of Paine, his suspicions are proven true in his mind. But then, when his life is totally spiraling out of control, Dixon meets Morgan, who offers him a chance to redeem himself. She detects his loneliness while he experiences an emotion he never knew existed. He realizes that the world is not the foul sty that he always thought it was and becomes willing to sacrifice himself for her. Morgan Taylor brings

love into Mark Dixon's life just as Laura Hunt brought love into Mark McPherson's life. But McPherson could have survived without Laura. Dixon wouldn't have had a chance without Morgan.

Initially, there appears to be a familiarity to Andrew's portrayal. He is his usual taciturn self, snarling his words when angry and spitting out others when impatient. However, there is also a suggestion of emotional instability, which Andrews projects through occasional twitches or a narrowing of his eyes. He also coveys repressed anger and simmering pain by the tightening of his lips and the increasingly hard tone to his voice. When he realizes that Paine is dead, his expression suggests panic and dread. Of the many scenes that reveal Dana's command of his character, the one in which Lieutenant Thomas discusses Paine's death is most illustrative. As Dixon listens to the details of the crime, his face reflects not only fear of being caught but a determination to keep his guilt hidden. The conflicting emotions of suppressed fear and self-contempt as he tries to pretend to be listening are all implied by his expressions. As Mark becomes increasingly desperate, his suffering becomes more evident but yet Andrews never resorts to overt displays of emotion. He continues to underplay, allowing the inner turmoil to reveal itself through his subtle changes in expression and the differences in his tone. As he responds to the love offered by Morgan, his demeanor

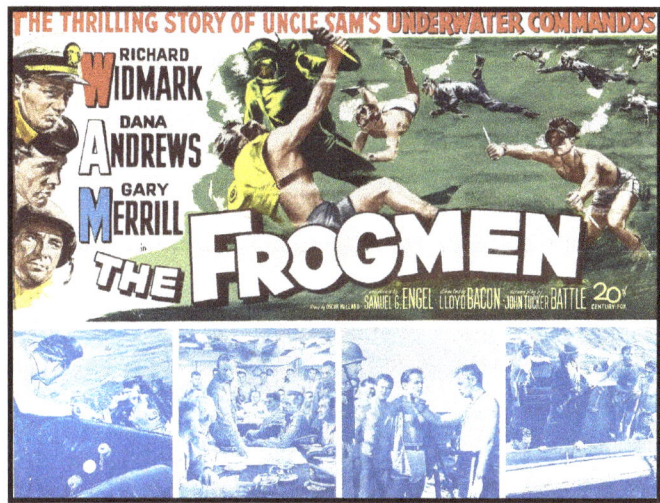

gradually changes. His reactions in her presence clearly suggest a softening from within that makes his redemption touching and believable. This is another superior performance by Andrews.

After 1950, Dana Andrews' career started to slide, due in part to his difficulties with alcoholism. Two more films for Samuel Goldwyn, *Edge of Doom* (1950) and *I Want You* (1951), were mediocre at best. A sign perhaps of his decreasing status was the fact that he had second billing to Richard Widmark in *The Frogmen* (1951), his last movie for 20th Century Fox (excluding a return to the studio in 1962). But he continued to work steadily throughout the decade at various studios, averaging about two movies per year. Another sign of his decreasing status was his appearance in 1954 in his first B movie in over a decade, *Three Hours to Kill*, a Columbia programmer. However, the movie emerged as an above-average example of the B-Western genre, due to his presence.

In 1956, he starred in two films for director Fritz Lang. *While the City Sleeps* (1956) is an underrated thriller about media manipulation and the hunt for a serial killer. The film noir aspects of the movie are illustrated by the manner in which the pathetic "lipstick killer" is contrasted with the newspaper people who appear to lack any semblance of morality in their determination to use the killings for their own ambitions. Andrews heads another fine ensemble cast as a reporter who is not above using his fiancée as bait for the killer. That same year Andrews also starred for Lang in a second movie, *Beyond a Reasonable Doubt*, which has a fascinating plot about a man who deliberately implicates himself in a murder, but the film is marred by having the appearance of a hurriedly made low-budget film. (It seems better today when compared to the terrible 2009 remake.)

In 1957, Dana re-united with Jacques Tourneur for another B movie, but this one turned out to be a British horror gem, *Night of the Demon* (U.S. title: *Curse of the Demon*). Andrews stars as a psychologist who investigates the death of a professor who had threatened to expose a mysterious doctor involved in the occult. Throughout the movie, the director's skillful use of his camera creates an overwhelming sense of menace, particularly in scenes that suggest malevolent forces may be hidden within seemingly normal surroundings. The movie gradually builds in suspense and terror as the cynical investigator is gradually forced to accept the reality of sorcery.

Andrews delivers another good performance as the skeptical psychologist, despite claims by some production personnel of his drinking during filming, as reported in Tony Earnshaw's book *Beating the Devil: The Making of Night of the Demon* (Tomahawk Press; 2005). Co-star Peggy Cummins' vigorous defense of Andrews negates this allegation, but the stereotype of the inebriated actor is too sleazy to resist by some petty people. Dana Andrews' alcoholism was a problem in his personal life during this period, as he would later admit, but he always refrained from drinking while working.

Dana Andrews plays a newspaper reporter, here with Thomas Mitchell, out to capture the "lipstick killer."

Peggy Cummins' assessment of Andrews' total professionalism is supported by the fact that Tourneur again worked with him the following year in *The Fearmakers*, the least interesting of their three collaborations. Furthermore, in the magazine *Little Shoppe of Horrors* #26, writer Denis Meikle exposes this rumor as a lie in his article on the making of the movie. Simply by viewing the film, Meikle proves that the producer's yarn of Dana's drunkenness during one pivotal scene is totally fallacious. Meikle writes that Dana Andrews "approached the role with all the skill of the Hollywood professional that he still was in 1956" and concludes that the movie "would have been only half the film that it is without him."

The appearance of the demon-monster has been a subject of controversy. Tourneur did not want the monster to be shown, but the producer demanded the puppet demon's inclusion. The producer wanted an exploitation movie that would attract teenagers, while Tourneur was aiming toward a more sophisticated audience. The mood of the movie is definitely affected by showing the monster at the beginning. Because of this, the viewer knows that the demon is real and that the occultist actually has supernatural powers. This prevents the identification with the psychologist that the viewer

Skeptical Holden (Andrews) confronts warlock Karswell (Niall MacGinnis) in *Curse of the Demon*.

should have. If the demon had been shown just at the end, the movie could have succeeded on both levels, as a monster movie and as an intelligent horror movie. As Tourneur had proven in his horror movies of the 1940s with Val Lewton, the power of suggestion can be more frightening than explicit shock.

In the 1960s, Andrews was the president of the Screen Actors Guild for three years. He appeared on many television anthology series and continued to appear in motion pictures, starring in programmers while also playing supporting roles in more prestigious productions. The year 1965 was an extremely busy one for the actor. He appeared in a total of eight movies, one of which was *In Harm's Way* (1965), his final movie for Otto Preminger and one in which he and his co-star from the 1940s, Henry Fonda, both had supporting roles. Other movies of the year included a starring role in *Crack in the World* and a supporting role in *The Satan Bug*. In *The Battle of the Bulge*, he appears for the last time with Henry Fonda, but he is fourth-billed to Fonda's top-billed role. The rest of the decade kept him equally busy.

Throughout the 1970s, the quality of Dana's film projects decreased, one exception being a supporting role in *The Last Tycoon* in 1976, which re-united him with Elia Kazan almost 30 years after their initial collaboration. He continued to work steadily in television, his presence adding old-fashioned Hollywood class to whatever project he chose to appear in.

Dana Andrews was one of the first actors to openly admit his alcoholism and, after achieving sobriety, made public service announcements for the government. He also gave speeches around the country to raise awareness of the problem. His generous work in this area gave courage and hope to many people who used his triumph over alcoholism as an inspiration for their own struggles. In addition, though he was very successful in real estate, he continued to act in occasional projects well into his 70s, until he retired due to health problems. He died at age 83 in 1992.

In most film references books, Dana Andrews is noted to be a Hollywood star of the 1940s and 1950s but is rarely referred to as a great actor. Nevertheless, in addition to being a very popular movie star, Dana Andrews was an extremely fine actor. His body of work is a testament to that claim.

Book Reviews
MAD ABOUT MOVIES
by Gary J. Svehla

Stoogeology: Essays on the Three Stooges edited by Peter Seely and Gail W. Pieper; McFarland www.mcfarlandpub.com; Order 800-253-2187; 280 pages soft cover, $35.00

The introduction of this book gives a succinct but thorough history of the comedy team, from Ted Healy through "Curly" Joe DeRita. Discussing the merits of Shemp vs. Curly and whether the team should have retired upon Curly's death, the introduction ends by asking the question we all ask. Superior comedic talents such as W.C. Fields, Buster Keaton, the Marx Brothers and Laurel and Hardy seem to have been forgotten, so why have the "lowbrow" Stooges "remained vital and contemporary"? The remainder of the book features essays that attempt to answer that essential question. Broken down into four chapters—"The Aesthetics of Stooge Filmmaking," "Stooge Psychology and Religion," "The Stooges Go to War," and "Race, Ethnicity, and Gender in Stooge Films"—19 illuminating essays try to explain the ongoing popularity and artistic triumph that comprises the Three Stooges essence.

Writer Peter Seely in his chapter on "Moidering the King's English: Puns, Wordplay, and Malapropisms in the Three Stooges Films," Seeley, demonstrating his skills as researcher, does something that McFarland seems to encourage. He creates chronological lists of dialogue with examples of wordplay featured in individual shorts. The lists go on and on for about 12 pages and document the cleverness of Stooge dialogue. However, such dialogue *sounds* funnier than it reads!

In the same writer's chapter on "The Surrealistic Stooges," Seely makes a strong case forwarding the surrealistic leanings of the Three Stooges' comic shorts. After both defining and offering a history of the literary term, Seely breaks the surreal occurrences in Stooges cinema into the following headings—Ghosts and Paranormal Phenomena; Traveling the Heavens and Beyond; Inhuman Beings; Manimals; Improbable and Impossible Circumstances; Time/Space Issues; Defying the Law of Physics; Inanimate Objects Coming to Life; Surrealistic Design; Hallucinations. Within each sub-division he gives vivid examples from the Stooges shorts to illustrate his thesis. So far the book, as you can guess, is rather scholarly and perhaps more cerebral than the comic team ever desired to be.

Along the same lines Tim Snyder gives us a chapter on "Deconstructing the Three Stooges: Freud's Concept of the Id, the Ego, and the Superego." The chapter defines each Freudian concept, using the personality of the Stooges as illuminating examples. Then Snyder offers broad examples based on each Stooge's distinct character, demonstrating how Curly represents the hedonistic Id, Moe the rational and orderly personification of the Ego and Larry, the voice of Stooge conscience, the Superego.

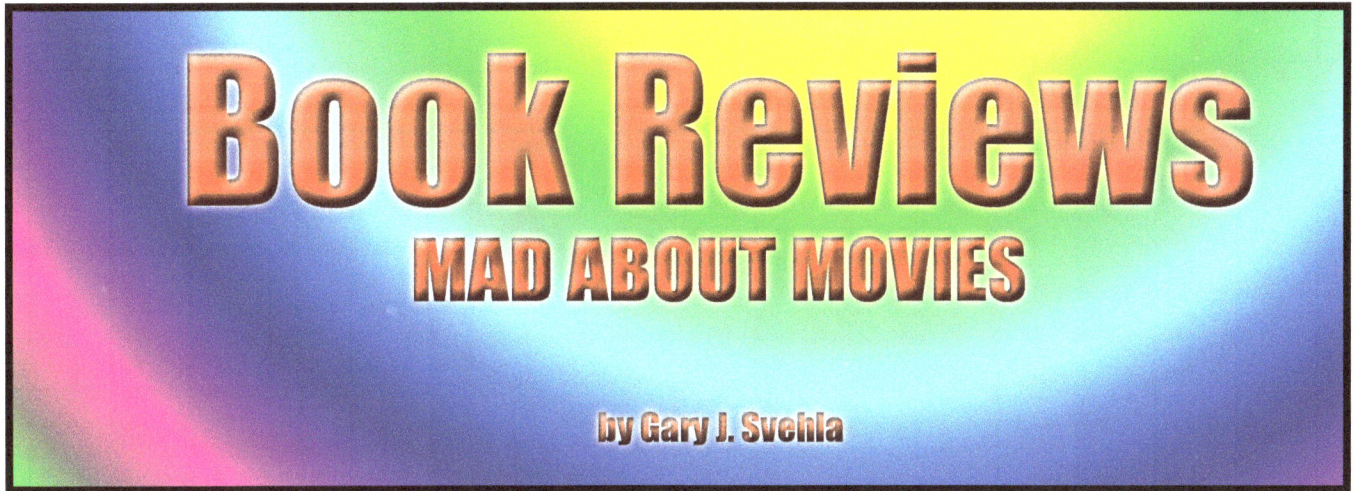

So far the authors seem to be justifying the Three Stooges as serious artists by applying pretentious concepts and academic framings to their shorts. Such an approach is worthy and often fun, but that approach forgets that the legacy of the Stooges flies against pretense and high art. For once the term "lowbrow" seems appropriate, much like a badge of honor.

For instance, in Lynn Rapaport's "Hang Hitler! The Three Stooges Take Potshots at Nazis," she focuses on the major Stooges shorts that feature WWII, Nazis and Hitler, *You Nazty Spy* and *I'll Never Heil Again*. But she also branches out, losing focus, by discussing the Stooges deal with Columbia head Harry Cohn, discussing portrayals of Hitler in general cinema, profiling other Three Stooges WWII shorts and going into a sidebar discussion of "Jewish Humor—Making the Enemy Small." All of this is well researched and interestingly written, but somehow the general sense of fun has been removed. These are Three Stooges *comedies*, let us not forget!

Ultimately, this is a book of serious criticism of the work of the Three Stooges. It is not a light-hearted romp for the casual fan. I found most of the essays intelligent, informative and thought provoking. Some of the writers perhaps read a tad too much into the Stooge insanity, but Moe, Larry, Curly, Shemp and the two Joes were artists who created their work over the course of many decades. Their creative output deserves such an exhaustive appraisal. But just lighten up a little, guys!

Anthony Mann: The Film Career by William Darby; McFarland www.mcfarlandpub.com; Order 800-253-2187; 304 pages soft cover, $39.95

Director Anthony Mann is one of the most important directors I *never* discovered as a kid. No, it took published criticism calling Mann's work quirky, left of center and idiosyncratic that forced me to gravitate toward his movies. When it comes to the second tier Western directors (after John Ford and Howard Hawks), Anthony Mann is frequently mentioned as being one of the greats, especially in his Western collaborations with James Stewart. But before his Westerns, Mann was praised for his work in film noir, frequently collaborating with gifted noir cinematographer John Alton. Later in his career, he helmed many epics and costume dramas. He died while working on *A Dandy in Aspic* in 1967. His movie career spanned three decades, Mann first becoming noticed as assistant director under Preston Sturgees on *Sullivan's Travels*. Film historian, fan and author William Darby, a college English professor, does a wonderful job detailing the film career of one of the most individualistic directors ever to grace Hollywood. Anthony Mann, refusing to be pigeon-holed or confined to one cinematic genre, became a true auteur, a director whose workman-like, journeyman productions only came to be seen as innovative and important after his death. Darby's style is always informative, fresh and interesting, never becoming too academic. At the same time his writing demonstrates original research and a perceptive viewing eye.

The book is broken down into many chapters including "In Search of Anthony Mann," "Mann and the B Film," Mann and Film Noir," "Mann and the Western," "Mann and the 1950s," and "Mann and the Epic Film." Simply from these chapter titles even the casual fan can see the wide range of movies that Anthony Mann made.

In the chapter on film noir, Darby approaches similarly themed noirs in two film discussions. So he pairs *The Great Flamarion* and *Raw Deal*, *Desperate* and *Side Street*, *Railroaded* and *He Walked by Night*, *T-Men* and *Border Incident*, but the historic costume noir *The Black Book* is examined alone. Darby establishes four basic scenarios/themes that appear again and again in Mann's noirs—blind love that leads to disaster or heartbreak; criminal involvement where the protagonist can only succeed by taking great risks; eccentric or charming villains; and police heroes who infiltrate the underworld. Darby's analysis is never convoluted and the manner in which he compares stylistic elements between similar movies is always effectively handled.

For many people, Anthony Mann hit his stride with his Western movies, classics including *Winchester '73*, *The Man From Laramie*, *The Naked Spur*, *The Tin Star*, *The Devil's Doorway*, *The Last Frontier*, *The Furies*, *Man of the West*, *Bend of the River* and *The Far Country*, all 10 Westerns produced from 1950 to 1959. Darby argues that unlike other Western directors of the time (Robert Aldrich, Delmer Daves and Budd Boetticher), "Mann fundamentally altered the emotional nature of the standard Western protagonist to provide a uniquely tragic atmosphere to the genre. The costs of preserving and protecting civilization, heroism through violence, and seeking revenge to right a damaged personal past are clearly laid out in the director's Westerns." And Darby does a terrific job explaining what works in each film and why, and he demonstrates the increasing complexity of Mann's moral universe (something first explored in his film noirs) as he made more and more Western movies.

I thoroughly enjoyed *Anthony Mann: The Film Career* by William Darby. Being a Mann fan for the past decade, not only did I learn a great deal about both the man and his work, but I also allowed Darby to connect the dots as Mann created major themes in his earlier movies and then sought to add further complexity to his ideas and themes, as his work matured. Always readable and enjoyable, this book comes highly recommended for any fan of the American Western and film noir.

DVD REVIEWS MAD ABOUT MOVIES
by Gary J. Svehla

Ratings: Excellent 4; Good 3; Fair 2; Poor 1

Act of Violence
Mystery Street
Movie: Act of Violence (3.0);
Mystery Street (3.0) Disc: 3.5
[Warner Bros.]

After the initial Warner Bros. film noir box set, which was excellent, expectations were high for forthcoming releases. However, with a few exceptions, Vol. 2 and Vol. 3 were slight and disappointing, especially when compared to the superior Fox film noir series. However, with Vol. 4, Warner Bros. is back in the saddle by releasing 10 features (on five single-sided double feature discs) that are definitely noir, definitely rare and definitely worth watching. And the entire box set sells on Amazon.com for $42, that's slightly over $4 per title. What a fabulous deal. And all the movies have been remastered and look vibrant in subtle shades of black, white and gray.

First up is the double feature of *Act of Violence* and *Mystery Street*. While *Act of Violence* was released on laserdisc, this is the first DVD release. And it's about time!

One strain of film noir focuses upon the lethargy of military men from World War II returning to their hometown civilian life, trying to pick up the pieces of their former lives and returning to a life of normalcy. *Act of Violence*, released in 1948, is one of the best. Contrasted are two returning veterans. The first is Frank Enley (Van Heflin), a contractor whose house-building business is taking off by leaps and bounds, and in his small town he is considered the ideal business and family man, loved by one and all. Enley is harboring a dark secret. He and his bombardier regiment were captured and held in a Nazi prison camp, but to save his own life, Enley spills his guts, and his men are massacred before an escape attempt. Every man dies except for Joe Parkson (Robert Ryan), who pretends to be dead but survives. Surviving but hampered by this betrayal and a weakened leg, our second vet Parkson lives only for revenge and firing a fatal bullet through Enley.

Director Fred Zinnemann, a few years before *High Noon*, creates a suspense masterpiece populated by noir shadows. Hiding a pistol under the jacket draped over his arm, Parkson rings the bell of Enley's home prepared to kill his former friend in cold blood, but Enley's wife Edith (a very young Janet Leigh) answers the door while watching over her infant baby, and she tells Parkton that husband Joe is up at the lake for a weekend fishing trip. Of course Parkson goes up to the lake, rents a boat and lies in wait to fire a fatal bullet, but fortunately he never gets a clean shot. When Enley hears a stranger has been asking about him, he packs up his gear and leaves abruptly and heads home, only to find out the stranger was at his house…and will return. During a wonderful sequence, the doorbell rings with all the lights in the house turned off, as Joe and Edith hurdle together listening for the gimpy man to walk around the back of the house and try to turn the doorknob, but the door is locked. Parkson returns to his car but simply sits and waits; he doesn't drive off. To increase the tension, the baby screams at the most peaceful times to startle the audience and make us jump.

During another sequence, Parkson follows Joe to a Builders' Convention and almost gets the jump on him, but Joe hides behind a column and suckerpunches the man and flees. Interestingly enough, Enley ducks inside a sleazy bar, about ready to close, where an aging, over-the-hill prostitute Pat (Mary Astor, who played the femme fatale in *The Maltese Falcon* only seven years earlier) offers Enley some comfort. Living in this quasi-underground world of small time criminals, Pat has a friend who will get Parkton out of Enley's hair, forever, for a price. Getting drunk, Enley, more in fear, encourages the thug to help him get out of this jam, but of course Enley regrets his decision the next morning. The film's climax occurs at the hometown train depot, late at night, where Parkson and Enley will finally meet; and Enley will finally earn redemption, but at a very high price.

The performances are uniformly strong, especially with the two male leads delivering intense, internal performances. Janet Leigh is wonderful as the kept-in-the-dark wife who loves her husband Frank to death. Mary Astor creates a marvelous supporting performance as a hooker who is both world-weary and worldly. In today's cinema she would be played by a hottie half her age, but Astor's

"Where is your husband?" Terror from the past stalks a happy home

performance is both intense, with her hard outer shell and her nurturing inner core creating a duality that holds our interest. Once we go beyond such a taut script, it is Zinnemann's direction that works closely with cinematographer Robert Surtees and makes the film memorable. More than a simple tale of revenge, *Act of Violence*'s moral ambiguity wrestles with the ethical choices of both men and sees virtue in each man's life. As Edith points out, Enley was weak and made a horrible decision, but he grew from that moment of weakness, married, became a great family man and community leader. At the current time he is not the coward that the war made him be for a split moment. On the other hand Parkton was an innocent victim justifiably outraged by Enley's cowardly actions, but after the war, Parkton's life is a wasted one, full of hatred and murder and little else. Parkson has not married, become a contributor to any community and appears to be little more than a drifter who lives only to kill. So who is the hero and who is the villain? And this psychological parable is framed as a tightly directed suspense thriller with the faithful family man on the run for his life, afraid to go to the police for fear that his past indiscretions will be exposed. And within this framework, even the crying of an infant can make the audience jump, as every shadow becomes sinister and every stranger lurking behind us might be, metaphorically, the violent past catching up with our civilized present.

Extras include an audio commentary track, trailer and a wonderful documentary where many critics comment upon the film's greatness.

Next up, the seldom seen *Mystery Street* is a police procedural that packs a wallop and provides a solid murder mystery by which to drape the film. The movie, filmed on location in Boston (and at Harvard University), has that urban realism but the scenery is not the typical New York or San Francisco setting. Boston has its own flavor, and in 1950 its setting was a novelty.

"B" girl Vivian lives at a boarding home run by snoopy Mrs. Smerrling (Elsa Lanchester), and when Vivian uses the hallway telephone to call a male friend who got her into a jam (i.e. she is pregnant), Smerrling listens in. The sizzling beauty wants her male companion to meet her at work, at the Grass Skirt bar, but the savvy two-timer asks the naïve bimbo to meet him near the secluded woods of Cape Cod. Needing a car, Vivian tags along with drunken Henry Shanway (a youthful Marshall Thompson), who is mourning his wife's hospital stay and stillborn birth. Seductively deserting Shanway in the middle of nowhere, Vivian confiscates the car, makes her rendezvous, but is shot and killed by her lover. In an interesting shot, when another car filled with teenagers drives by, the killer cuddles the still-warm corpse of Vivian and pretends to be making out with her alongside the car. Then, in a scene reminiscent of *Psycho*, the cloaked fiend drives the car with the corpse inside into a lake, totally submerging the vehicle.

Six months later bones wash ashore and Lieutenant Morales (Ricardo Montalban) and Harvard forensic scientist Mr. McAdoo (Bruce Bennett) join forces to identity the victim and put the fragments of the case together. Serving as a precursor to today's *CSI* and *Bones* TV series, *Mystery Street* is quit masterful in piecing the puzzle together. Such procedural science is presented dramatically and with tension, so the pacing does not drag.

Veteran performer Elsa Lanchester is marvelous as the conniving landlady, a woman who remembers the phone number that Vivian called the night of her death, and she traces the number to the address of a shipbuilder, one James Harkley (Edmon Ryan), a sleazy businessman who just happens to hide the missing murder weapon, a .45 caliber automatic pistol (the newspaper identified such a missing weapon), in his locked desk drawer. Smerrling, while Harkley is detained, searches the office and places the weapon in her purse, returning later with blackmail in mind. The subtle repartee between these two is delightful, with each person's greed and evil one-upping the other. In the typical blackmail deal, Harkley offers the woman $500 for the gun, but she holds out for $2,000. When Harkley comes to her apartment to finish the deal, he bashes out her brains with a metal candlestick holder but escapes without the gun, eluding the police who are in hot pursuit. It seems the gun is being held at a train depot baggage claim area, but even though Morales finds the claim ticket, they want Harkley to claim the bag and get caught with the murder weapon in his possession. The climax occurs on the train tracks as Harkey, bag in hand, dashes in between trains, ducking on and off train cars, until he breaks the bag open and fetches the gun, which he must destroy to protect himself. In the final conflict, Morales and Harkley (who made a crack earlier about his family being in America for 100 years contrasted to Morales' recent immigrant status), go one-on-one against each other.

While Sally Forrest's performance as Shanway's dutiful wife is grating, the other major performances, especially Elsa Lanchester, Marshall Thompson and Edmon Ryan, shine. The movie's plot is always interesting, with what at first appears to be minor little sequences soon adding up to something major. The direction by John Sturges is moody and suspenseful, complimented by the wonderful on-location black-and-white photography by John Alton. For a seldom seen film noir, *Mystery Street* is a true delight.

Extras include another short but interesting documentary, trailer and audio commentary.

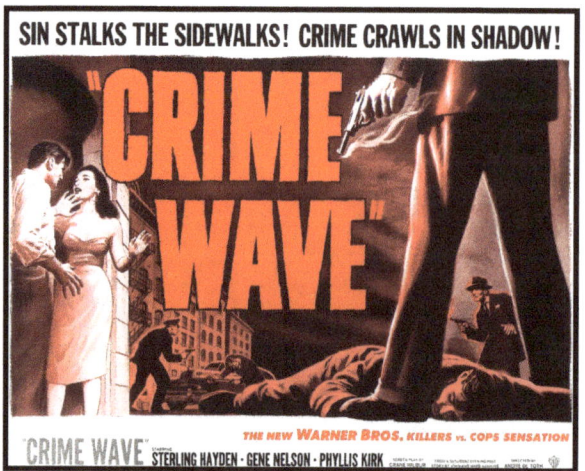

Crime Wave
Decoy
Movie: *Crime Wave* (3.0); *Decoy* (3.0);
Disc: 3.5
[Warner Bros.]

One of the delights of the Warner Bros. Film Noir Collection 4 is its wealth of little-known noir gems, such as the two included on this double-feature disc. The first, *Crime Wave*, filmed before *House of Wax* by director Andre De Toth but released afterward, is considered by many to be De Toth's finest effort. Certainly, after multiple viewings, *House of Wax* seems more and more generic, lacking a distinct style. Not so *Crime Wave*, which is dripping with thick noir overlays. First up are the major stars, ex-con Steve Lacey (Gene Nelson), trying against all odds to go straight, and his wife Ellen (Phyllis Kirk, who would work next in De Toth's *House of Wax*), trying to keep him out of jail. Ellen is the dominant (yet quietly sexual) partner in the marriage. The wonderful Sterling Hayden plays the tough-as-nails police detective Sims, a man who towers over everyone in the movie (the imitation documentary cinematography style usually films Hayden with low-angle shots, looking up at his hulking presence). Citing the doctor making him give up cigarettes, Sims chews toothpicks by the gross. He is a cop who snaps out dialogue in rapid-fire sentences, hates the grimy criminal underground of L.A. and mostly does not believe that ex-cons can go straight. What he thinks and feels mostly remains hidden beneath a veneer of crusty arrogance and world-weariness, but his character is the emotional center of the film.

Second, and most importantly, these rich characters populate a world of grit and decay, both in the criminal system and the police system, allowing De Toth's direction, aided by the cinematography of Bert Glennon, to bring this world to rancid life. Economy of filmmaking best sums up De Toth's style. Take the first few minutes of the movie, (filmed on location) detailing a night time gas station robbery by three criminals (Charles Buchinsky, aka Bronson, plays one of the more violence accomplices). The thugs club service attendant Dubb Taylor from behind and push his body beneath a counter, and when a motorcycle cop surveys the scene and stops to investigate, another criminal shoots him. As the still-walking cop races in front of the gas pumps, he is shot again, falls on his belly and still has enough strength to attempt to crawl to his motorcycle and police radio. Sadly, he dies before he reaches his destination. One of the robbers,

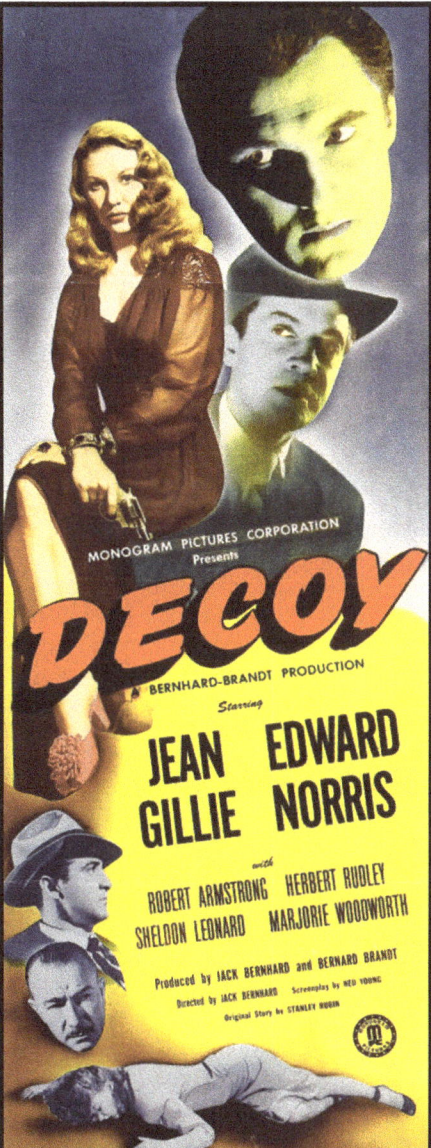

seriously wounded by the policeman, is given most of the money (less than $200) and a car to escape. The other two criminals will fend for themselves. Of course the wounded thug goes to the home of Steve and Ellen, and tells Steve an animal hospital doctor will arrive shortly to treat him. When the wounded man dies, the vet takes off, leaving Steve Lacey with the body. Steve phones his parole office to avoid trouble, but trouble still arrives as the police, including Sims, come upon the scene. Before long the rest of the gang invades the Lacey home and forces the ex-con to become the driver for their next ironclad error-proof bank robbery, and Steve agrees although he is only doing it to protect his wife. What none of the gang knows is that Sims and his men are on to the robbery and that policeman will be placed in the bank, posing as bank tellers and bank office workers, when the robbery occurs.

Gene Nelson plays Steve Lacey as a humble man caught between two worlds, but he's anchored more toward the world of morality because of his faithful wife. Lacey drives a souped-up deuce coup and sometimes becomes a James Dean poseur with his black leather jacket and full head of hair. Sims seems to hate the ex-con, but a surprise at the end proves the ambivalence of feelings that exist between the cop and the con. The movie, at the standard B length of 74 minutes, is gripping because of its tight editing, wonderful characterizations and direction. Extras include another brief documentary with plenty of impressive talking heads, and the audio commentary includes author James Ellroy (writer of *L.A. Confidential* and *The Black Dahlia*) whose noir literature typically occurs in the Los Angles of the late 1940s and 1950s (and *Crime Wave* was filmed in 1952 where it sat on the shelf on two years, awaiting release), so this on-location cinematography has Ellroy waxing ecstatic as he recognizes the various locations. Film noir expert Eddie Mueller does most of the work, but Ellroy is fascinating by his outrageousness and passion for L.A. noir. *Crime Wave*, as the two claim, provided a template for Stanley Kubrick's *The Killing*, also starring Sterling Hayden in basically the same role, a few years later. For me discovering this lost noir oddity only emphasizes how essential such releases are.

Also on the same disc is another forgotten gem, this time a Monogram Picture released in 1946 and "introducing" British cult actress Jean Gillie to American audiences (she would make only one more film before her untimely death). Directed by Jack Bernhard, *Decoy* is another B programmer (coming in at a brisk 76 minutes) whose plot steals threads from other, better film noir productions. But as this patchwork quilt unfolds, the movie's success relies chiefly on the stellar femme fatale performance by Gillie (who perhaps becomes one of the coldest woman in the history of noir), the moody cinematography and the film's eccentric yet clever framing story narrative.

Can film noir boast a better opening than *Decoy*'s? It begins with a pair of dirty hands soaping up and drying off, over a disgustingly filthy gas station washbasin. The man exits looking as white as death and ambles on totally zoned out. Thirty years later we might describe him as a living-dead zombie from a George Romero production. Asking for a lift from a gregarious driver, the passenger stares blankly ahead, ignoring both the conversation and jokes made by

the kindly driver. Soon the man is let out in the city, where he ambles up the elevator in a ritzy apartment building, heading for a specific destination. Knocking on a door, the barely breathing man enters the apartment and approaches Margot (Jean Gillie), a woman he knows, and he parts his sports jacket to show her his bloody chest riddled with bullet holes. He takes out his pistol and plugs the defenseless woman, and he falls to the floor dead. Margot, mortally wounded, awaits the entrance of police detective "Joe-Joe" Portugal (Sheldon Leonard), who gently carries the woman to her sofa. In flashback she retells the story that leads to this point in the film.

At the movie's end, after the caper, scam and double-cross is carried out (with Margot's ruthless actions appearing at every turn and playing men for suckers at a steady clip), we return to Joe-Joe and Margot, with the cop reading the signals that, even if on opposite sides of the law, they should kiss. Onlookers watch as Joe-Joe bends over to kiss the sizzling beauty. Margot breaks the mood by laughing out loud sarcastically, making a total fool of the cop, before she dies as she finishes the story. What a cold bitch!

The plot twist involves (how's this for science fiction film noir!) criminal mastermind Frank Olins (the always wonderful Robert Armstrong) refusing to reveal where his stolen fortune is hidden. Olins goes to the gas chamber, but afterwards Margot reveals that if a chemical antidote is administered one hour after death, the chemical will bring the dead back to life. And as soon as Frank returns to the living (Armstrong delivers an amazing physical performance as the shocked, re-animated human) and draws a map which he splits in half, keeping half for himself, Frank returns to the dead with an unsuspected bullet in the back. The next victim (what good is a femme fatale without the slobbering male pansy), in this case a poor but honest prison doctor (Edward Norris), agrees to go along with Margot's plan, more for the potential sex than the money. After he helps Margot recover a buried wooden chest of $40,000—down on his knees pushing the crate toward her—she shoots him twice in cold blood, leaving him for dead in the woods, alongside the state highway. But as the beginning of the movie attests, he is far from dead.

For a poverty-row Monogram Picture, *Decoy* is wildly outrageous and effectively made. The film's chief ace-in-the-hole is the mesmerizing Jean Gillie, whose innate evil makes her an unforgettable femme fatale. Her performance becomes the film's reason for being and remains ingrained in our minds long after the film ends. Her "I got you" laugh to poor Sheldon Leonard as she lies dying is one of the defining sequences in film noir history. Extras include an audio commentary track, another effective documentary (with plenty of impressive talking heads, including Dick Cavett) and a trailer.

The Big Steal
Illegal
Movie: *The Big Steal* (3.0);
Illegal (3.0); Disc: 3.5
[Warner]

In this stellar continuation of the Warner Bros. Film Noir Volume 4, we have archetypal, brooding noir anti-hero Robert Mitchum, returning to RKO after his marijuana bust and re-teaming with Jane Greer, his co-star from one of the noir classics, *Out of the Past*. *The Big Steal*, directed by upcoming hotshot director Don Siegel (*Invasion of the Body Snatchers* and *Dirty Harry*), has less the dark film noir tone of *Out of the Past* but more of an on-the-road romantic relationship flavor. The script by Daniel Mainwaring (as Geoffrey Homes) is slight and doesn't bear up under intense scrutiny, but the acting and visual momentum more than make up for that weakness. Mitchum plays Duke Halliday, a lieutenant accused of stealing payroll money from the military, and Halliday tails an oily criminal named Jim Fiske (Patric Knowles) down to Mexico. Fiske probably possesses the stolen money. In hot pursuit is perennial noir heavy William Bendix as Captain Blake, the military man out to arrest Duke and retrieve the missing bounty. In the meantime Halliday crosses paths with the lovely Joan Graham (Greer), who was engaged to the rascally Fiske before he hit her up for $2,000 and ran away. Both Halliday and Graham trace Fiske to his hotel room, while the crook once again slips away. They both hold Fiske's map that they believe marks the hidden spot where the stolen treasure might be. Before long the Mexican police, under the direction of Inspector General Ortega (Ramon Novarro), becomes involved in the hi-jinks and decide to tail all these suspicious Americans running around Mexico.

The Big Steal becomes one long chase, either in pursuit of Fiske and the people he works for, or eluding the determined Captain Blake, who won't give up his pursuit of Halliday. Interesting sequences include Halliday and Graham, on the road, their car just moments ahead of Blake's, unable to pass slow-moving locals who block the narrow, dusty road. When Halliday gets clear, he encounters local Mexicans digging a drainage ditch in the road, and they lose even more of their advantage. Formulating a story about eloping and being chased by a shotgun wielding father, Halliday gets

the road crew to use boards to build a small bridge that Halliday can use to cross over the repair work, all of which suddenly vanishes when Blake approaches. In another sequence Halliday and Graham get the drop on the smarmy Fiske, and Halliday leaves Graham holding the gun on Fiske while he searches Fiske's car. Of course Fiske declares his love and outrage and asks how could she take a stranger's word over his. Graham is not able to fire her weapon, allowing the con man to back her against the wall, grab her gun, slap her face hard and lock her in the closet. Fiske slips away once again before Halliday returns.

Such sequences lead to the explosive climax where we discover that Fiske is working for another man, a man whom we believe to have been honest throughout the entire film, but a man who easily explains the disappearance of the money and the frame of Halliday. Another insignificant character turns out to be the fence for the stolen money and the only solution is for the criminals to do away with Graham and Halliday, but such simple solutions do not exist in the world of *The Big Steal*.

The Big Steal is a solid noir, not a classic along the lines of even the overrated *Out of the Past*, and while Greer and Mitchum sizzle and their relationship propels the scenario, Jane Greer is transformed from the sexual predator of *Out of the Past* into a much more plain and polite beauty. Even though she has a shower scene, hardly anything more than a bare shoulder can be seen. Her flirtatious lines of dialogue entice more than her body language is ever allowed to communicate. And Robert Mitchum, by the late 1940s, has begun to morph into his apathetic screen persona with the hangdog face that ushered in the decade of the rebel-hero a few short years later. Extras include the standard documentary featuring hordes of interesting experts and a trailer.

Next up is a wonderful remake of a 1930s film, *Illegal*, starring Edward G. Robinson in one of his best under-the-radar roles. Released in 1955, directed by Lewis Allen (*The Uninvited*) and scripted by W.R. Burnett (screenwriter of *High Sierra, This Gun for Hire*), *Illegal* plays to the stereotype that all lawyers are politically motivated and self-serving. Edward G. Robinson is wonderful in the splashy role of D.A. Victor Scott, a self-made man who rose up from the city slums to become the city's top-dog lawyer. Telling his young friend Ellen (Nina Foch), a fellow attorney in the D.A.'s office, that his goal has always been to use his office to become governor, Victor Scott is ready to grab the brass ring and achieve his goals.

Then in a second, all is lost. Scott convicts an *innocent* man (a youthful DeForest Kelley) and sends him to the electric chair, and immediately after, when the victim's innocence is revealed, Scott's prime seat at a high-class restaurant is no longer available and his political friends ignore the blackballed man. Scott resigns as District Attorney and realizes his role of becoming governor is shot to hell. He turns to drink and sinks from higher class bars to dives, soon opening a private practice and becoming a defense attorney, using gimmicks and ploys to win his cases. In one dramatic court case, Scott drinks a vile of potential poison to make the point that poison is not in the vile, but no one in court knows that the poison does not work for 45 minutes and that a well-planned recess will allow Scott the time to prance slowly out of court and be attended to by a medical team who has the antidote ready to inject. Robinson's performance as Scott is one bravura moment after another, but soon Scott finds himself becoming the right arm of criminal kingpin Frank Garland (Albert Dekker). The new D.A. suspects a leak from his office, and since Ellen enjoys a very close father-daughter relationship with Scott, the D.A. suspects Ellen of being the leak. However, Ellen's finance Ray Borden, who also works in the D.A.'s office, turns out to be the informer. Ellen catches the truth in a phone conversation that Ray has with the criminals, and when Ray tries to silence Ellen permanently to keep his identity hidden, Ellen must shoot and kill him. But the D.A.'s office still sees Ellen as the leak and prosecutes her as the murderer who killed her lover when Ray found out whose side she was working for. Of course Victor Scott defends her in court, struggling to prove his case even though a fatal bullet has ruptured his gut as he bleeds to death in the courtroom. But the wily attorney, who must win this case, cannot afford to miss a beat.

What a wonderful, over-the-top film noir, a film that is splendidly acted by one and all. Besides Robinson, Edward Platt ("Chief" from the *Get Smart* TV series) is cold as steel as the new D.A. and Nina Foch walks that fine line between loving Victor Scott as a father and as something more. Hugh Marlowe is excellent as the younger man that Scott tells Ellen to marry, but a man who gets into trouble with gambling and has to pay off his debts by becoming a mob informer. Albert Dekker plays the gentlemanly mob boss very subtly and never goes over the top. Jayne Mansfield debuts as his moll, a stereotypical beached-blonde bimbo, but one with real acting talent.

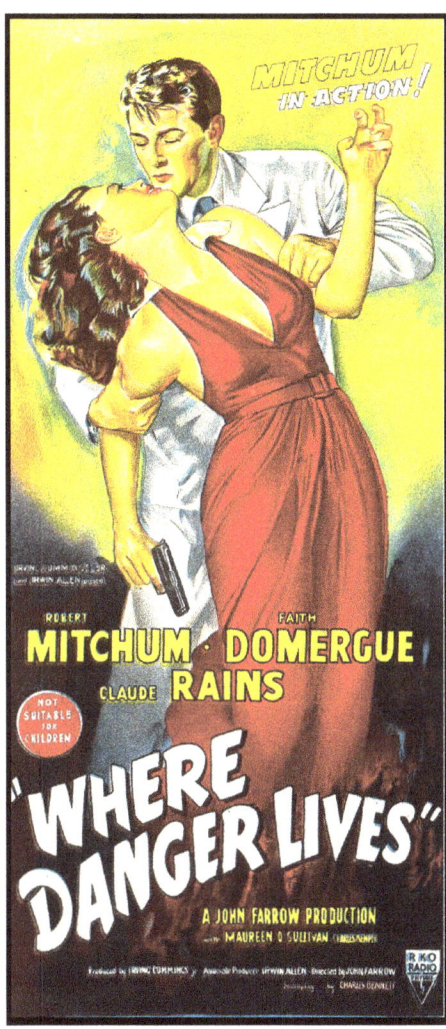

Mansfield appears throughout the movie in a minor part, as she strums at the piano and sings the type of classic pop standards that Frank Sinatra was about to make famous on his 1956 release, *Songs for Swinging Lovers*.

Illegal works so wonderfully because Edward G. Robinson is allowed to create such an effective, broad performance. As Victor Scott he starts off arrogant and proud. Soon he descends to a skid row has-been, disappointing his former friends and co-workers. He rebounds but does so by becoming the type of lawyer that gives the legal profession a bad name. His star rises again, but at the expense of personal morality and good conscience. But by the movie's end, mortally wounded, he regains his soul and vision of a defender of the people. Dramatically, as he lays dying in a court of law, the judge expresses the hope that he will see Scott defending victims in his court soon. Seldom has film noir been this much melodramatic fun. As usual, a documentary appears, a trailer and as a special bonus, Edward G. Robinson's interview appearance promoting the film is also included.

Where Danger Lives
Tension
Movie: *Where Danger Lives* (3.0);
Tension (3.0); Disc: 3.0
[Warner]

One thing always stands out about Robert Mitchum. No actor is better able to symbolize the film noir malaise and nadir tone better than he, and *Where Danger Lives*, another double-feature disc in the Warner Bros. Film Noir Collection Vol. 4, shows why. The 1950 RKO film, produced when Howard Hughes was running the studio and promoting the various young actresses with whom he was having affairs, shows the strengths and weaknesses of such a formula. Mitchum is memorable once he gets clunked over the head, but is far less believable early on as the pompadoured doctor (Dr. Jeff Cameron). Too much of the good-bad-boy pouting lip and white-jacketed physician emerges, and it's no wonder that the nude-beneath-the-sheets Faith Domergue (as Margo, an iconic film noir name), apparent suicide-attempt victim, gets her mojo sparked by the sight of the doctor. She wants to live again! Yes, this is hokey.

However, the rich playgirl and the humanistic doctor (his first scene occurs as he comforts a child with polio in an iron lung) fall head-over-heels in love, but Margo stymies a romantic trip saying her father insists she go on vacation with him. Armed with a single rose (the original title was *White Rose for Julie*, Julie being the nurse that Cameron works with and the less sizzling beauty [played by Maureen O'Sullivan] that truly loves him), Cameron goes to Margo's mansion to surprise Margo and instead meets the tense but friendly Frederick Lannington (Claude Rains), the so-called father figure. Cameron states his intentions to marry Margo when the coy and sophisticated Lannington announces he is Margo's husband, not her father. With an all-knowing smile Lannington announces she got wealth and he got…youth (and he refuses to grant his wife a divorce). In total shock and embarrassment Cameron leaves to the tones of Lannington talking about knowing the true Margo, but Cameron returns when he hears a scream and finds Margo wounded. Soon Lanningan picks up a fireplace poker and attacks Cameron, who punches Margot's husband unconscious. Wishing to call the police, Cameron is dazed by a poker blow to the back of his head, becoming disoriented. Leaving the room to wash up, Cameron returns to find Lannigan dead, but did he die from the aftermath of the punch or did Margo assist in her husband's

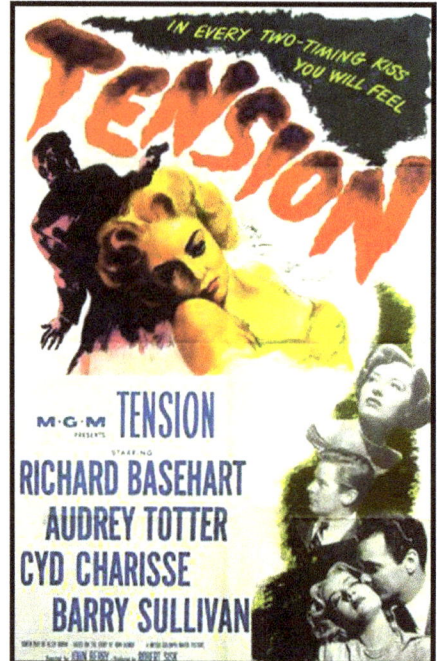

demise? The film then becomes a cat-and-mouse chase film, with the lovers evading the authorities, Cameron making all sorts of bone-headed decisions, all due to his bump on the noodle. However, as Cameron diagnoses his condition as being a severe concussion, he warns that he will become light headed, pass out, go numb in his extremities and eventually sink into a coma from which he may never awake. Margo becomes equally erratic herself.

Here's a flaw of the movie. While Mitchum is too James Dean for the physician role, for most of the film he becomes merely a criminal on the run, a victimized and physically ill one at that. And Mitchum's Howard Hughes' squeeze Faith Domergue, while beautiful in an off-kilter way, never becomes quite believable. In some sequences she purrs or pleads a little too deliberately and her eventual insanity perhaps emerges a little too quickly, without enough subtlety. It is more a performance of attitude without depth. While her femme fatale is always interesting, her performance does not take full advantage of the bravura potential. Claude Rains, billed third in what is little more than a cameo performance, excels at what he implies but does not say. In a sense the elder Lanigan knows his wife is a psychopath, a sexual meteorite that will incinerate any man with whom she becomes involved. Before Lannigan can tell Cameron the whole story, Margo silences him forever by smothering him with a pillow off screen so we never know the truth until the film's climax. Then, in typical film noir style, the almost crippled Cameron, wobbling down the street, confronts the escaping Margo, who tries to shoot him, and as Margo attempts to cross the Mexican border, an unforgiving border patrol militia confronts her.

While flawed, the relationship between these three makes for a dandy film noir that sizzles with sexuality grounded in insanity. Under John Farrow's focused direction, the film deals with the obsessive love a physician holds for an evil and mentally ill siren. *Where Danger Lives* is melodramatic film noir at its most sinewy and raw. Extras include a trailer, audio commentary and a talking-heads documentary. This film noir box set is loaded with insightful expert commentary.

Tension, perhaps the lesser of the two films, is another seldom seen noir mystery thriller that is loads of fun. Produced in 1950 and directed by John Berry, the film provides a showcase performance for rising-star Richard Basehart in another hokey scenario that works in spite of itself. Iconic femme fatale Audrey Totter, bleached blonde, her full figure filling out her scant skirts and droopy tops, plays Claire Quimby, wife to four-eyed nerd Warren (Basehart). He manages a drug store trying to support Claire in the type of life she desires, but she cheats on him with a burly hedonist Barney (Lloyd Gough), who lives the extravagant party lifestyle. Claire leaves him for Barney and the nebbish little man is shattered emotionally.

Ah, but here's the contrived plot thread that becomes fun in spite of it being preposterous. Nerdy Warren, donning new fangled contact lenses, concocts a new identity with a spiffy wardrobe and new look. Calling himself Paul Sothern, Warren rents one apartment with his new identity as a traveling salesman and befriends the lovely Mary Chandler (musical star Cyd Charisse). In her first shot, Charisse, famous for possessing some of the finest legs in showbiz since Betty Grable, straddles a fence and gate as she stretches to take a photograph. Mary becomes the girl who loves Warren/Paul and their budding relationship sustains the needs of both parties. But Warren cannot leave well enough alone. Craving revenge and wanting Claire back, the dapper Paul sneaks into Barney's house at night to kill him, using his new identity as his alibi. However, at the final moment he allows Barney to live, but he drops a pipe-cleaner man that Mary made for him. And of course when Barney is found murdered, the police (Barry Sullivan and William Conrad as wonderfully insightful and intense police detectives) quickly uncover the dual identity scenario and put the finger on Warren, but even when the police take Mary to the drugstore to identify Warren, she plays her hand very coolly and does not tip off the cops that Warren is actually Paul.

In an interesting twist, Barry Sullivan's Lt. Bonnabel, who appears throughout the movie stretching a rubber band (the central symbol of the "tension" of the title), appears to be developing a physical attraction to Claire. During the film's climax when Claire breaks into the Paul Sothern apartment to plant the murder weapon, it appears that Bonnabel might even be in on the scheme to frame the innocent man. But as he pulls the rubber band further and further apart, Bonnabel surprises everyone with his shocking revelation that forces Claire to show her hand, to prove her guilt. And at the end Mary figures out that Bonnabel was buffing and merely grasping at straws to prove Claire's guilt and exonerate Warren.

Tension succeeds mainly because of its performances, especially the almost dual personality performance submitted by Richard Basehart (who was handsome in his younger days), but the conflict stems mostly from the tension created by the warring females, with Audrey Totter's performance a smothering standout and "whose sneer of cold command," as Lord Byron once wrote, says it all. Totter, like Elvis, could use her quivering lower lip to speak volumes. And the almost Dragnet-style performances by Sullivan and Conrad (with a crueler edge) only embellish the goings-on. *Tension* features an audio commentary (featuring Totter), trailer and featurette.

**They Live By Night
Side Street**
Movie: *They Live By Night* (3.0);
Side Street (2.5);
Disc: 3.5
[Warner]

In 1949, Farley Granger and Cathy O'Donnell shined an unheard of romantic light on the film noir genre by playing the young, doomed lovers in director Nicholas Ray's first feature, *They Live By Night*. The film opens with a very strange prologue that introduces the young stars and their characters, with a shaky helicopter shot that follows a speeding car down the highway. The car houses three escapees from the local prison camp. Two of them are hardened career thieves, Chicamaw (Howard Da Silva) and T-Dub (Jay C. Flippen), but one of them is a 23-year-old innocent, a boy held in prison since he was 16 years old. And there's the impetus for the story…will the young innocent stick to his plans to make enough money to hire a lawyer to prove that he never received due process at age 16 and be freed, or will he succumb to the criminal influence, harden himself against the world and continue his life of crime? As the vets tell Bowie (Granger), they got him out of prison for one reason, to become the third man in their bank robbery gang, reminding the boy that it takes three to rob a bank.

Chicamaw takes the gang to his brother's isolated farm to hide out and regroup, before engaging in a pattern of brash bank robberies. Mobley (Will Wright) is happy to shelter his brother and friends, but he is a hopeless drunk whose teenage daughter Keechie (O'Donnell) lives a life of isolation. She has become a well-trained auto mechanic who dresses in a mechanic's uniform with simple combed-back hair. In her first sequence, driving to pick up the ankle-sprained Bowie, who is hiding out off the highway, O'Donnell appears more like a guy who shyly offers the energetic boy a ride. Slowly, she begins to dress more as a girl when she is around him and in her awkward way flirts with the handsome male, offering to run away with him. In a wonderfully acted sequence, they fall in love or something close enough for each of them. Keechie confesses she's never been around boys and does not have experience kissing any (the sexual implication stings deeper than the kissing reference), and Bowie admits his own lack of experience with girls (he was arrested at age 16). So both of these awkward and isolated country youths slowly reach out to one another and try to build a relationship of love and trust, based upon the assumption that Bowie will abandon his life of crime. But Bowie realizes that Chicamaw and T-Dub won't simply abandon their third clog and that he needs a nest egg to bring to the marriage.

The film is based upon the novel *Thieves Like Us* and that title becomes a running theme throughout the movie. Bowie believes in the moral code of honor among thieves; lawbreakers need to stick together and help one another out (such as Mobley taking in his outlaw brother and friends). However, the film constantly brings home the point that everyone has some kind of angle and that everyone, even the so-called honest folks, are thieves, even if they exist on the "right" side of the law. The wedding chapel proprietor Mr. Hawkins (Ian Wolfe) best represents that symbol. Keechie and Bowie go to his chapel to get married at 12 midnight, and he quickly offers them the $20 basic service or the enhanced $30 service. They settle for the $20, and in a rushed but professional manner, the kids are married. Realizing the sordid background of the young lovers, Hawkins offers them a chance to get to Mexico…for a price. And he offers to sell them a car, for a special price, with $500 going directly to him for his efforts. In other words, Hawkins is cordial and professional, but he is also ready to make a profit from the misfortune of others. By the film's explosive ending, Bowie sneaks back to the chapel to take Hawkins up on his offer to get the couple to Mexico, but he states glumly he only sells deals where there's at least a little ray of hope. Knowing now that Bowie is outlaw "Bowie the Kid" and is marked by the law, he tells the boy that he cannot sell them any hope, so the deal for Mexico is off. And following the theme of the movie, Mattie, a sleazy woman who is friends with the outlaw element, turns over the whereabouts of Bowie to the police, in a deal to exonerate her friend and herself. Bowie, naïve and still trusting her, asks Mattie for paper and pencil to write a note to Keechie, telling her that he loves her, but that he must head out on the road for a while. Mattie, who runs a roadside motel, pretends to be sheltering the young couple, and Bowie thanks her for all her help…stating people like us must stick together. But little does he know that the police are laying in ambush outside his motel room when he exits to say good-bye to Keetchie (egged on by Mattie, no less).

Even the media gets the facts wrong, playing up Bowie the Kid as the ringleader and brains behind the outfit, incensing Chicamaw who relishes the fame and adoration that the outlaw life brings. He does not want to play second banana to the kid in newspapers across the nation.

Obviously, Arthur Penn based a good deal of his classic *Bonnie and Clyde* on *They Live by Night*, especially the climatic finale where betrayal leads to the deadly ambush and Bowie's death, as poor Keetchie runs out of the motel and cuddles her dead husband, backing away and mouthing the message written to her in his note which she finds in his pocket…"I love you," as the end titles appear. *They Live by Night* offers little new to the criminal noir genre, but with a wonderful script co-written by director Nicholas Ray, the film offers two innocents caught up in a corrupt world who momentarily find a little peace and comfort in one another, putting their love affair front and center. And that's a taste of something new to film noir, making the film a little different. Extras include a featurette with the usual talking heads, trailer and audio commentary, featuring Farley Granger.

The second and certainly lesser Farley Granger and Cathy O'Donnell film noir, *Side Street*, is also one that is rarely seen today. This 1950 on-location New York City noir (the film opens with wonderful aerial shots of New York City that are breathtaking), directed by quirky director Anthony Mann, becomes film noir for the Everyman, the typical working-stiff who comes front and center in the screenplay. As the voiceover narration tells the audience, Joe Norson (Granger) is neither the hero nor the bad man, he is a typical "Joe" who works part-time delivering mail to businesses (after having lost his gas station and moving with his wife into her parents' home). Joe stops and smiles to admire the fur coat in the store window he wishes he could afford to buy for his wife Ellen (O'Donnell), who is pregnant and about ready to deliver. However, because of finances, she must attend a public city clinic and this embarrasses Joe, who wishes so much more for his new family.

Poor Joe. This is a noir and he is ready for temptation and corruption, all in the name of providing for his family. When he visits a lawyer's office to deliver mail, he interrupts a telephone conversation between the lawyer Victor Backett (Edmon Ryan) and his mistress who are blackmailing her lover for $30,000. The sap pays the money and the lawyer's "muscle" George Garsell (James Craig) delivers the incriminating photos and negatives. Too-busy Joe does not follow any of the phone conversation, but he sees two $100 bills on the floor that George scoops up and places in a metal file cabinet. So, of course, the next time Joe delivers the mail and the office is empty, he uses a fire-extinguisher axe to break open the cabinet and steal the folder that houses the money. What Joe doesn't know is that the folder now holds $30,000 blackmail money and not the paltry $200 dollars. When Joe opens the folder upon a rooftop hideaway, he now does something equally stupid…he takes the folder, now wrapped up as a present for his wife, and asks his local bartender to hold the package, behind the bar, until next week for him. When next week arrives, the bar has been sold to a new owner, the old owner is gone, and the package, still hidden behind the bar, is now minus the money.

It is not long before Backett and Garsell and their gang figure out that Joe stole their ill-gotten gains, but without the money to return, Joe must evade his pursuers. At the same time he must try to trace down the thieving bar owner and recover the $30,000. While the unsuspecting Ellen lies in the hospital giving birth, Joe visits her briefly and then disappears, trying to restore his perfect life as the gang decides to take Joe for a little ride during the climax.

Most film noirs feature heroes that are at the crossroads of society, barely sufficient detectives or nightclub owners who have on-going relations with the criminal element, ex-cons trying to go straight and even policeman who battle personal demons to travel the straight and narrow. Here, with *Side Street*, the establishment of a working class Joe is an attempt by Anthony Mann to bring the noir aesthetic to the average citizen, the average man who tries to make ends meet but comes up short. Yes, the character of Joe Norson should have better sense, and if he thought the situation through, he never would have acted as he did. But this fabricated inner turmoil becomes the dramatic impetus that fuels the plot, and even if Joe's motivation becomes somewhat cheesy (*Side Street*, while of interest, is perhaps the least of the 10 noir features presented in this collection), the innocent man on the run frame always produces interesting results. Cathy O'Donnell's part is minimal and her performance consists mostly of her pleading eyes, wishing Joe to be safe. Farley Granger perhaps gets too carried away playing an innocent young-married caught in a trap, but his good heart overcomes his stupidity so the audience always pulls for him, right up to the very end of the movie. The usual extras appear, including the featurette.

The Hardy Boys:
The Mickey Mouse Club
The Mystery of the Applegate Treasure
Movie: 3.0; Disc: 4.0
[Disney]

When I was a kid, back in 1956, I can remember watching *The Mickey Mouse Club* on TV every weekday afternoon. While I enjoyed the antics of the Mouseketeers with their songs and dance, the adventure serials stick out most vividly in my mind, with *The Hardy Boys: The Mystery of the Applegate Treasure* and its infectious theme song becoming a vivid childhood remembrance. I always loved the mysteries, and even later with *The Wonderful World of Disney/Color*, I always gravitated toward the whodunits.

Think of more recent examples such as *Goonies* and the *Harry Potter* series, and we see that mysteries and juveniles go hand-in-hand. However, even with detectives that are barely in their teens, the basic plot must be sophisticated enough so that adults can still be captivated by all the shenanigans. *The Mystery of the Applegate Treasure* succeeds on all these levels. Besides the teaming of Disney perennials Tim Considine and Tommy Kirk in the roles of the thoughtful Frank and boisterous Joe Hardy, we have interesting sidebar characters including Arthur Shields (who one year later would star in *Daughter of Dr. Jekyll*, with John Agar) as the gentleman crook, Boles. In fact his outrageous, over-the-top performance is so slick and entertaining that he becomes the standout in the entire serial. Florenz Ames as Mr. Applegate is another eccentric but standout character. Even the dotting Sarah Selby as Aunt Gertrude and Robert Foulk as Jackley submit fine character turns.

Interestingly enough, all the exteriors are actually interior studio sets (the Applegate backyard, with mountains of earth dug up, the water tower, the Hardy house and even the street on which they live) allowing the juvenile actors to film extended night sequences during the day (because studio sets could be light controlled). Thus the Disney world of the Hardy Boys becomes a marvelous wonder-world of haunted mansions, bell towers, foreboding neighborhood streets, old apartment buildings and suburban woods.

Disney created such episodic adventures to be played as basically 10-minute serials (each chapter introduced by the catchy title tune, which became slightly repetitious by the final few chapters) that played four weeks on *The Mickey Mouse Club* (as a segment that was incorporated into the hour-long show). So in 1956 the chapter-play was still alive and well at Disney, even if each chapter was basically half the length of the typical serial chapter (but *The Mystery of the Applegate Treasure* consisted of 19 chapters). What made the series so gripping was the suspenseful musical score (created by William Lava) and the cinematography (by Gordon Avid and Walter Castle). Whether we encounter Mr. Applegate charging at the boys with his cutlass in his spooky backyard or we are part of the hysteria when the police are banging out the walls in the upper levels of Applegate's home, searching for the pirate's treasure, all the pieces of the puzzle fall into impeccable place (the imaginative art direction by Bruce Bushman and Marvin Aubrey Davis is essential). Basically the well-crafted plot by Jackson Gillis remains true to the literary source and holds both youngsters and adults in a web of suspense. Of course being able to see the serial in one sitting (even though we cannot avoid those damn musical beginnings) only demonstrates what a fine piece of family-oriented filmmaking *The Mystery of the Applegate Treasure* is, as the serial holds up to even tougher scrutiny today.

Sold in a collector's two-disc tin, *The Hardy Boys* appears with pristine restoration, looking sharp and dense in its black-and-white photography. The original hour-long *Mickey Mouse Club* show that premiered the serial is included, as well as marvelous intros by renowned Leonard Maltin. Also included is a documentary on *The Hardy Boys* literary series and its conversion to Disney moviemaking, and finally, an interview with Considine and Kirk concludes the excellent package.

Perhaps revisiting this Hardy Boys package is so warm and cozy because I remember it from the fuzzy days of my youth (I was six in 1956), but I have a feeling that any fan of 1950s cinema and Disney in particular will enjoy this excellently scripted and acted youth serial. Hey, it doesn't have the bang of the *Harry Potter* series but as a lower-budgeted adventure mystery, it still connects and creates smiles. Like revisiting *Leave It To Beaver* (before we saw the reruns and box DVD sets too many times for our own good) for the first time, *The Hardy Boys*, less remembered and seldom seen in recent years, remains fresh and entertaining and captures an era in America that is so nostalgic today. I cannot wait for more serials to be released from Disney.

Lost City of the Jungle
Movie: 3.0; Disc: 3.5
[VCI]

Universal is primarily known for its Flash Gordon serials, which are highly lauded and considered among the best serials ever produced. However, *Lost City of the Jungle*, although a very flawed serial, still demonstrates that in 1946 the studio still knew how to produce an exciting chapter play.

Horror star Lionel Atwill is billed third in the credits, and most genre fans are attracted to this serial because of Atwill's villainous performance. Even more tragic and interesting is the fact that Atwill died during the middle of production and the studio had to rewrite/recut the movie to salvage the sudden death of its chief villain. Script-wise, the serial is a mess with clunky story changes made, information retold multiple times and sequences filmed hastily featuring an actor (who hunches down and pulls a big floppy hat over his face) substituting for the sadly departed Atwill. These replacement sequences are almost as ridiculous as the similar sequences with Bela Lugosi's double filling in for him after he died while *Plan 9 From Outer Space* was still in production. Atwill's death really screwed up the effectiveness and quality of this serial. However, even with all this re-thinking, re-cutting and re-shooting, *Lost City of the Jungle* still thrills, entertains and holds audience attention.

The plot involves the birth of a new worldwide peace organization, after the end of World War II, whose purpose is to prevent power-hungry maniacs from starting another war. The organization sends agent Rod Stanton (Russell Hayden, an actor who played sidekick to Hopalong Cassiday in many of his B-Western entries) to a small country at the base of the Himalayas, Pangrang, where he will join already situated Tal Shan (Keye Luke) in discovering the world-destructive plans of evil mastermind Sir Eric Hazarias, who operates with a new identity and appearance. Hazarias intends to penetrate the dense jungles (tropical jungles at the base of the Himalayan mountains?) and find the source of new radium that could be used to create atomic weapons and protect the user from harm. It seems Pangrang is ruled over by an opportunistic woman Indra (Helen Bennett), whose interests are mostly personal and financial, and she manages to wiggle between and work with both Hazarias' people and Stanton and Shan. As the serial develops and Hazarias' agents try to double-cross and deceive Indra, she finally sides with the agents of the peace organization and

comes to realize that her little nation cannot afford to remain isolated.

The man introduced as Sir Eric's secretary, Malborn (John Mylong), is revealed to be the big brain that challenges the authority of his boss Sir Eric, but never to Sir Eric's face. When agents appear to report their findings to Sir Eric, often Malborn will state, "You can tell me, of course." Basically, when Atwill was ill and left the production, the role of the villainous sidekick must have been rewritten to make the personal secretary a major henchman, but at the same time, Sir Eric remains the main henchman since his star appeal sells tickets. In other words, the plot had to be re-crafted to have a new main villain after Atwill left the production, and while certain sequences could awkwardly be covered with a double, others simply needed the inclusion of an actual on-screen villain who could interact with other characters. So Sir Eric remains in charge and is unaware of the deceptive practices of his colleague. After establishing Malborn as the brains of the operation, henchman Johnson (Dick Curtis) shoots and kills Malborn unceremoniously in the next to last chapter, when Sir Eric decides he no longer needs his secretary.

Atwill appears chipper and hardy in his sequences, which are too infrequent for fans of his villainy, and is able to look dapper and deliver his lines with the proper gusto and evil subtlety. If the serial had been finished with Atwill, the horror celebrity would have had much more screen time and the opportunity to chew up even more of the scenery. His death simply had a profound effect on the final cut of the serial and lessened its impact.

However, the expensive art design and set direction, and the antics of the heroes and the professor/daughter team of Ted Hecht and Jane Adams (who starred as the leading lady in *The Brute Man* and played the sympathetic hunchback nurse Nina in *House of Dracula*) carry all these shenanigans along with excitement and gusto. Unlike the Republic serials, fistfights are used sparingly and not to ridiculous ends, where the hero gets beat up in every chapter. And unlike Republic serials where gunplay is used sparingly and no one gets shot, let alone killed, here in the world of Universal serials characters do get shot (sometimes by the heroes) and sometimes even die. These serials seem more directed at an adult audience where anyone can get injured at any time. Also, the complex plot is not an easy one for children to decipher.

The serial contains many exciting cliffhangers that only enhance the suspense and thrill quota. In one chapter finale our heroes are in a speeding boat, the villains in front of them flinging hand grenades back at them. As the chapter ends, Rod Stanton is fishing for a grenade in the back seat of the boat, when it explodes, throwing splintering wood sky high. Of course in the next chapter, we see Stanton and Shan jump into the water *before* the explosion. Perhaps in the best cliffhanger finale, the lovely Jane Adams is tied to a chair that is propped in front of a mantle where two bookshelf elephants slowly approach one another. A rifle emerges from the wall and is ready to fire one shot into the center of the chair where Adams sits, when the elephants meet. As the chapter ends, our heroes are fighting out in the hall as the professor and his daughter struggle to escape their binding ropes. Suddenly we close in on the mantle as the rifle lowers its sights and fires. Next chapter we see how Stanton, at the very last possible second, lunges into the room, knocking the chair over on its side, as the rifle discharges. Another chapter ends with our hero's head in a guillotine in the middle of the jungle, and the blade descends and lands with a loud thud. No doubt this cliffhanger holds audience attention.

With stars such as Lionel Atwill, Keye Luke and Jane Adams, *Lost City of the Jungle* is exciting going all the way. The plot might be too convoluted and complex for its own good, and the lack of Lionel Atwill is always a detriment, but the action is tense, the settings exciting and the thrills continuous. Not one of the greatest serials, but *Lost City of the Jungle* is a cinematic expedition worth taking. The serial, as is typical of VCI, is pristine and dense. Extras include a few trailers and on-screen bios of cast and crew members.

The House on Telegraph Hill
Movie: 3.0; Disc: 3.5
[Fox]

Robert Wise saw this film released in 1951, the same year his classic *The Day the Earth Stood Still* reached the screen, so this was, creatively, a very fine year for the director. *The House on Telegraph Hill* is a mystery noir of the best type, conforming to the successful formula of having an innocent young woman move into a dark mansion, with plenty of skeletons in the closet, and falling in love with a handsome yet dark and brooding man who becomes her husband. Soon, spooky occurrences occur and the audience (and woman) is left to wonder, who exactly is this man she married?

Director Wise, who is an old hand at these types of stories, adds the element of a double deception. During the closing years of WWII, two Polish women, suffering together in a concentration camp, vow to weather the storm and help one another along. Karin is the far weaker one, but she must survive to be reunited with her nine-year-old son Chris, who is being cared for by Karin's aunt in San Francisco. Her friend in the camp, Victoria (Valentina Cortesa), steals food and medicine to keep Karin alive, but Karin succumbs to her environment and dies. Victoria has nothing to return home to, so she steals Karin's identification papers and decides to assume her life. However, before she leaves the camp she learns that the elderly aunt has died and that relative-by-marriage Alan Spender (Richard Basehart) has assumed guardianship of the boy. Victoria journeys to San Francisco to meet Alan Spender, and before long, she marries and moves into the mysterious house on Telegraph Hill.

Victoria/Karin loves the splendor of her new home and bonding with the child that she pretends is her own. Falling for the handsome Alan is an added plus. But it isn't long until Victoria, playing catch in the backyard with Chris, stumbles through the thick bushes and discovers a shed, a playhouse, mysteriously left abandoned, sporting a huge hole that looks downward over the side of the rocky bluff. Chris refers to an explosion from a chemical play set years ago, but strangely, the accident-waiting-to-happen still remains un-repaired. Also, Alan seems to be very close, perhaps too friendly, with nanny Margaret (Fay Baker), a woman who parades around the house alluringly after hours, sometimes spending time alone with Alan. Margaret seems very protective of the boy and often contradicts Victoria's wishes. At this same time Victoria becomes reunited with the soldier who aided in her freedom from the concentration camp, Major Bennett (William Lundigan), a lackadaisical playboy that seems attracted to the already-taken wife of his buddy Alan. When Victoria's car's brakes fail, the car descending the hilly San Francisco streets, causing her to crash, she begins to suspect her husband wants her dead. Along about the same time, Alan approaches his wife in a spooky sequence, while she is in the shed, his abrupt approach forcing her to walk backwards, nearer and nearer the dangerous hole in the floor, resulting in her tripping and almost falling to her death (Alan coming forth to rescue her at the last moment). So Victoria seeks shelter in the arms of friend Major Bennett. Alan, who seems kind and concerned about Victoria's mental health, makes the young wife doubtful of her own fears of him. But when Victoria breaks into Margaret's personal locked journal does Victoria discover that the aunt was alive when her letter was received but she was dead only days later, thus heightening her fears about her husband's motives. And then she is confronted with an innocent glass of nighttime orange juice delivered by her husband, with a special glint in his eye, Victoria realizes that all her fears may be justified.

Wise's direction makes use of his decade-earlier horror film tricks, showing Victoria's first evening in the house and her restless night, spooking us with the silhouette of a monstrous tree branch banging against the window of her bedroom. In close succession Victoria wanders off alone toward the dark corridors of her newly found mansion home, only to be startled by sounds from closed-door rooms and finding her husband and Margaret emerging from one of them. At the movie's end, we never see Alan pour Victoria's orange juice, but behind the wall we clear the clink of a spoon stirring the glass (unnecessary if the orange juice is merely orange juice), that sound suggesting unmentionable horror. In the brilliant sequence in the shed when Alan approaches his wife, as she backs up in total fear, the audience is never clear about his intentions. The stark and contrasty photography makes his silence threatening, and the way he is photographed as emerging from the black shadows makes him appear terrifying without actually doing anything horrific. The ambivalence of this sequence only demonstrates why Robert Wise is such a craftsman. *The House on Telegraph Hill* takes its place along other mysteries of the era such as *The Spiral Staircase* and *Sorry, Wrong Number*, but in the hands of master Robert Wise, the film's subtlety and psychological undertones add a richness and resonance that transcend the B formula. This film can be watched over and over again.

Fallen Angel
Movie: 3.0; Disc: 3.5
[Fox]

Otto Preminger produced and directed a film noir classic with *Laura*, but most of the old noir magic is gone with *Fallen Angel*, nonetheless, it is still a noir worth seeing. Dana Andrews, one of *Laura*'s stars, is back, joined by a strong cast including Alice Faye, Charles Bickford, Bruce Cabot, John Carradine and the sizzling Linda Darnell as Stella. While *Laura* featured a complex, multi-layered plot, *Fallen Angel* is simpler and far less satisfying.

Basically, a PR company owner, Eric Stanton (Dana Andrews), who lost his company due to unlucky gambling habits at the casinos, is kicked off a bus heading toward San Francisco and stops in a stopgap dusty town. Stanton heads towards Pop's to have a beer. Everyone assembled, including Pop and a retired policeman, await the return of waitress Stella, a hottie whose taste in men is anything but exemplary. When the sizzler finally returns to make a dramatic entrance, the camera stops dead in its tracks, approximating the sexual explosion that Kathleen Turner created in the equally provocative *Body Heat* (1981). But for 1945, Darnell was pure sexual tension and her entire all-too-brief performance reeks of sexuality of the most wildly abandoned type. Stanton is smitten with her, but she does not seek mere male companionship, she wants that ring and a man who can provide for her. Thus, he befriends and soon marries the prettier of two spinster sisters who set themselves up as the moral compass of the town. Stanton, being careful when abandoning his wife June (blonde and attractive Alice Faye, but sexy in a proper and cute manner) on their wedding night to seek out Stella at Pop's, wants access to naïve June's safety deposit box in Frisco, but for honor's sake he avoids sexual intimacy with his wife. Finally, when Stella turns up dead, killed by a sharp blow to her temple, Stanton is suspect number one. His wife's total commitment to her husband, even willing to give him her nest egg and ignore his physical attractiveness to Stella, results in Stanton beginning to fall in love with

of the vulnerable, broken man and also is a crafty opportunist who takes advantage of situations by deceiving those easily fooled. June Mills, as played by Alice Faye, is woefully undeveloped and the audience wishes to know more what's occurring within the character's mind. She sometimes seems totally naïve, but at other times her insight and understanding of her husband is almost uncanny. But for the 1940s, Linda Darnell as Stella is one of the most carnal creatures of the decade, and even though her part is far shorter than we might wish it to be, her performance lingers for a long time.

Fallen Angel is slightly slow moving, but its lazy character study of desperation, sexual obsession and redemption is an interesting ride, subtly helmed by master Otto Preminger.

14 Hours
Movie: 2.5; Disc: 3.5
[Fox]

In 1951 the on-location film noir subgenre, the *policier* or procedural film, was quickly, and unfortunately, catching on with Hollywood. People at this time were perhaps very interested in knowing just how the F.B.I tracked down their man and how the police operated behind the scenes. And in *14 Hours*, the interest here is how the New York police deal with the problem of suicidal jumpers. What might have been of keen interest back in 1951 is not quite as interesting today, and while the procedural nature of the film is not necessarily a flaw, but if it dominates character and plot, then we have a problem.

Over all *14 Hours* is suspenseful, expertly photographed by noir master Joe MacDonald (his high and low angle shots of the hotel at night, big spot lights illuminating the side of the hotel, are gripping) and effectively acted overall. However, the dramatic tension created by the jumper has been done so many times, and often better, that the film loses momentum about half way through. Richard Basehart plays attitude and emotion and does it well. His Robert Cosick is a man teetering on the edge, a man who hates his father and whose mother (Agnes Moorehead) is such an emotional, whining mess that we collectively want to slap her. Cosick keeps reminding us that his father drinks too much. The psychiatrists who oversee the operation love to throw some ready-made Freud our way and their pop-shrink lessons are too pat. The people in the street do what we expect them to do—one group of gentleman bet on the hour he will jump. A young Debra Paget and Jeffrey Hunter, attractive young people, are glued to the streets fearing that the victim will jump, and Paget's Ruth keeps reminding us how sad the man looks (and he's up on the 15th floor of a hotel!). However, the image of these two people, a typical girl and guy, who don't know one another, ends the film as they walk away from the hotel, hand-in-hand, obviously romance is blooming and made possible by Cosick's threat to jump.

Most admirable about the production is the terrific performance of Paul Douglas, who plays the common Joe traffic cop, Charlie Dunnigan, the man whose blue-collar sincerity wins over the despondent Cosick. Dunnigan has not been trained to save the lives of jumpers, but he is the first man on the scene, and after his superiors send him home, Cosick requests that Dunnigan be called back. As the affable policeman sits on the window's edge, a piece of rope tied tightly around his leg if he gets the chance to grab Cosick, the conversation becomes the heart and soul of the production. The relationship even develops to the point that the good-hearted cop, who truly wishes to help this stranger, invites the man over to his home to meet the wife and have dinner. Today in our cynical world such a conversation would never happen, but in the purer 1950s American culture, the way strangers reach out to one another (the Debra Paget-Jeffrey Hunter romance of strangers vs. the Dunnigan-Cosick sick souls in need of healing relationship) is emotionally moving and makes us long for those more innocent days.

While *14 Hours* is at best okay, some of its performances (including a small cameo by Grace Kelly, who plays a woman meeting her lawyer to go over the terms of her divorce … another allusion to a broken relationship) transcend and make us wish for a movie that would better stand the test of time.

Michael Shayne Mysteries: Volume 1
Movies: *Michael Shayne: Private Detective* (3.0);
The Man Who Wouldn't Die (3.0);
Disc: 3.5
[Fox]

Michael Shayne, starring Lloyd Nolan as the grizzled and sexed-up private dick of pulp literature, came to 20th Century Fox during the 1940s in a hardboiled-light version that made the series a perfect way to spend a Saturday afternoon. It is wonderful that now the lesser detective and mystery series are being brought to DVD, and many long-forgotten programmers can once again be enjoyed.

In the first entry, *Michael Shayne: Private Detective*, Lloyd Nolan establishes the private detective as a slightly rough-around-the-edges yet highly likable Joe. While the tone of the movie, like the Charlie Chans, is never too dark or hardboiled, it does tend to veer toward the comedic at times. Shayne, as portrayed by Nolan, is self-deprecating and he often makes mistakes. In one pivotal sequence, Nolan takes a phone call in his office as his furniture is being repossessed. As insensitive movers empty his file cabinet, throwing all his records haphazardly on the floor, Nolan is presented with a case that will offer him cash immediately, but the detective realizes the shady morality of the deal offered, and even as his livelihood is being carted away, with steadfast moral fortitude, he refuses the case. Stalling for time with the offer of another case, Shayne delays the movers who are waiting outside, but when he can only offer the men the promise of money, they continue to carry out chairs and desks.

Shayne, who is hired to keep tabs on a young, wild and free high society girl, who has a taste for the gambling table, Shayne attempts to teach her a lesson when he fakes the death of her criminal gambling boy friend, who is left drugged and unconscious at the steering wheel of his car out in the boondocks, ketchup smeared over his shirt. However, after phoning the police to further enhance his playful tease, Shayne takes Marjorie (Phyllis Brighton) where the car is parked, and together they see that the body now has a gunshot wound to the head and he is actually dead. Of course Shayne's fired gun is at the scene of the murder, and the police sirens sound after Shayne helps Marjorie escape, while his own car stalls.

Marjorie's crackerjack Aunt Olivia (Elizabeth Patterson) provides the comic relief, and she energizes every sequence in which she appears. Aunt Olivia is a fan of Agatha Christie mysteries and prides herself on solving all the mysteries before the resolution is revealed in the final rapidly-turning pages. When it comes to an actual real-life case, Olivia is ready to teach Shayne a thing or two, and the repartee between the two makes the movie shine even brighter. For once the comic relief is quite intelligent and well acted. Such antics actually add to the overall quality of this debuting entry. But Lloyd Nolan remains the main reason to watch the film, as his take on the typical hardboiled private detective is both playful yet witty. Extras on this first disk include a fascinating documentary giving the history of the Brett Halliday fictional series and how it eventually evolved into a movie franchise.

The second Michael Shayne entry, *The Man Who Wouldn't Die*, is also the shortest title in the set, coming in at 65 minutes. Most noteworthy is the lush black-and-white cinematography by Joe MacDonald. MacDonald photographed some of film noir's finest moments: *Pickup on South Street, Niagara, The Street With No Name, The Dark Corner, Shock, Call Northside 777*, etc. Here, in the opening minutes of the movie, MacDonald struts his stuff. In glorious, shimmering black-and-white shadows, MacDonald films several men as they cart a corpse out the front door of a lavish mansion, and a beautiful but worried blonde looks on from the doorway. The corpse is stashed in the back of a car and driven to a wooded burial ground where, in a most amazing pan, the camera crosses the faces of all concerned as they stare down at the makeshift grave. Minutes later a dark, shadowy figure returns to the mansion, his eyes illuminated by two small spot lights, where he enters a woman's bedroom and starts firing his weapon in her direction, before fleeing. The fact that the condition of this print is pristine and superior to the first Shayne entry always helps the effectiveness of the photography. But instead of the more hardboiled approach to the first Shayne, this entry plays up scientists in cellars, adds the old dark house mood with twisting corridors and rooms within rooms and mysterious phantoms haunting the wooded grounds.

Marjorie Weaver is back from the first film, again playing a spoiled rich girl, but this time she is called Catherine Wolff. Catherine hires Shayne to pretend to be her husband, a man she only just married, so Shayne can help to solve the case involving the man in the shadows who fired pistol shots at her while she slept. Lloyd Nolan, who disappears for about 15 minutes of the 65 minute-programmer, returns later but dominates every sequence in which he appears. Whether he is singing an old Irish ditty or overwhelming Cathy's stern father with his charm and sense of humor (the old man thinks "husband" Shayne only married his daughter for the family fortune), Shayne is a bombastic sleuth who uses his bright personality more than his detective skills. One of the best sequences is when Shayne and Cathy explore the dank basement and find a hidden laboratory used by Dr. Haggard (Henry Wilcoxon) to extend the life of mortals. Shayne straps himself into the experimental chair and accidentally turns on the electrical apparatus, giving himself a *Man Made Monster*-style charge that almost kills him. The sequence is played for humor, yet the Kenneth Strickfadden-derived electrical contraptions create a true horror film feel, and of course Joe MacDonald's inspired photography only helps establish this tone of terror.

The plot evolves that the buried corpse in the movie's opening sequence doesn't stay dead, even when he is killed again in a fiery automobile crash, and even when Shayne says his head has been crushed, the

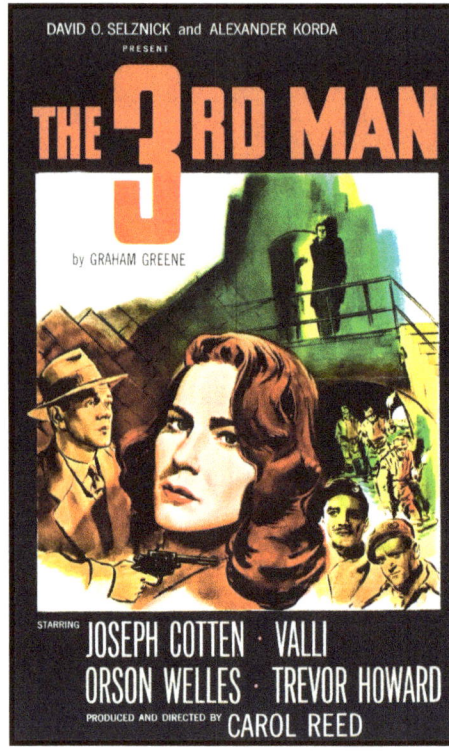

corpse somehow manages to escape from the morgue unscathed and returns to the mansion for one last night of horror.

The Man Who Wouldn't Die has more of a series feel than *Michael Shayne: Private Detective*. The movie assumes we already know the character of Shayne and little time is spent reacquainting the audience. The style of this entry has changed from gangster to old dark house mystery, which only shakes up the ingredients and adds more interest and surprises. Lloyd Nolan continues to create a thoroughly entertaining detective hero, one that manages to make a few mistakes and even act cowardly once in a while. Yet, when it comes to solving the mystery and saving the day, Nolan's character does just fine. The documentary extra features an interview with the illustrator of the sexy and lurid Shayne paperback book covers, and a gallery of his covers illustrates his pulp sensibilities.

Completing the collection are two additional entries—*Sleepers West* and *Blue, White and Perfect*—two effective B programmers worthy of the first two films, once again demonstrating that such typically forgotten detective series of the 1940s are well worth checking out.

The Third Man
Movie: 3.5; Disc: 4.0
[Criterion]

Criterion recently reissued the Carol Reed British classic *The Third Man*, remastered as a two-disc set (or a single disc Blu-ray disc, with all the extras).

In many ways, *The Third Man* is overhyped and for me never quite lives up to its reputation. Don't get me wrong, it is one of the better film noir entries and contains perhaps the best noir cinematography ever, masterfully photographed by Robert Krasker, with its use of two-story high shadows of Harry Lime absolutely iconic. While most of the photography occurs on location in Vienna, many studio sets (including the underground sewer system) were constructed and incorporated into the actual location photography.

The Third Man works best during the initial hour, before Harry Lime (Orson Welles) is introduced (he only appears during the film's final 38 minutes), when the movie functions as a noir mystery. Joseph Cotton plays Holly Martins, a pulp writer of Western stories, who goes to occupied Vienna (at the end of World War II) to be the guest of best friend Harry Lime. Upon his arrival Martins finds himself at Lime's funeral, as he was the tragic victim of a hit and run auto accident. Two friends at the accident scene claim that Lime either died instantly or spoke a few sentences and then died. But a porter, whose building overlooks the accident scene, tells Martins confidently that there was a mysterious third man present on the scene. Martins' quest to find that third man and through him the cause of Harry Lime's death is the impetus of the drama. Complicating matters is Lime's beautiful lover Anna (Alida Valli, who also appeared in the classics *Eyes Without a Face* and *Suspiria*), with whom Martins slowly falls in love. She has been using a forged visa to remain in Vienna (now governed by four Allied powers in the aftermath of WWII) because she is actually a citizen of the Soviet Union. The British military at first wants Martins out of the country, but soon they feel they can use him as a decoy to lure the perhaps not dead Lime out of hiding. It seems gangster Lime smuggled illegal doses of penicillin into Vienna and sold it on the black market, but in diluted variations that caused children agonizing deaths or left them permanently impaired.

During the first hour we think of Lime as a devilish and stylish rogue anti-hero, clever enough to stage his own death. Once Lime appears we learn of his horrible criminal activities that harm children, and we discover that Lime was working with the Soviets to expose his lover Anna, to deport her, so Lime would be left alone. Anna still loves Lime, but Martins knows the deception afoot and protects Anna from the harsh facts. Lime is a slimeball, and somehow the truth makes him less the iconic anti-hero the audience expects.

Lime's dashing introduction is a classic of cinema. Walking down the dark, shadowy Vienna streets, Martins spies a silhouetted figure standing in the shadows of a doorway, a perky cat at his feet. Lime emerges from the shadows, streetlights illuminating him, as the camera focuses on his sly (and arrogant?) smile, which seems to communicate…"Ha, ha, ha, I am still alive!" It is a wonderful introduction, but the subsequent scenes feature Lime not quite so confident. Lime asks Martins how the authorities know about his resurrection. From the moment Orson Welles opens his mouth the audience dislikes him.

The climatic chase through the Gothic sewers of Vienna makes for a classic set-piece of pulse-pounding proportions. As the police climb down manhole covers and close off all avenues of escape, we watch as the rodent-like Lime hovers in the shadows, climbing up ladders, scurrying down wet passageways, seemingly trapped, yet somehow he eludes his pursuers. One of the film's chief flaws is the simple fact that, although a criminal, audiences still like Harry Lime. A pivotal sequence telegraphs that Lime will be forced to shoot a policeman the audience likes, and this turns the tide against Lime, so pal Holly Martins will be seen as a clean-cut hero when he confronts his friend and shoots him to death. This dramatic aspect seems a tad mechanical and manipulative.

Perhaps the best sequence in the movie occurs at the very end, mimicking a similar sequence from the film's beginning, showing Martins in a Jeep leaving Lime's funeral (the fake one at the beginning, the actual one at the end), driving down the same dusty road, and passing the depressed, grief-stricken figure of Anna, as she walks stoically alone down the road. The sequence is shot exactly the same both times and the players perform it exactly the same emotionally. However, at the film's end, Martins forces Major Calloway to let him out of the Jeep, giving him one more chance to win back the heart of Anna, difficult now that he shot and killed her lover. At this solemnly bleak setting, the movie ends.

The Criterion collection contains two documentaries (one 90 minutes; the second 30 minutes); audio commentary; two radio dramatizations, including the classic *Lux Radio Theatre* presentation with Joseph Cotton. Other extras are also included, making this package a definitive one to own The blu-ray disc image is gorgeous!

www.ingramcontent.com/pod-product-compliance
Lightning Source LLC
Chambersburg PA
CBHW051350110526
44591CB00025B/2959